101 Tips
—— for ——
More Profitable
CATALOGS

101 Tips
for
More Profitable
CATALOGS

Maxwell Sroge

NTC Business Books
a division of NTC Publishing Group • Lincolnwood, Illinois USA

Cover Acknowledgments (Clockwise beginning upper left)

From the *Summer of '89 Tweeds* catalog. Courtesy of Tweeds, Patterson, New Jersey. Used by permission.

This spread is from the *L.L. Bean™ Winter Sporting Specialties 1989* catalog. Copyright 1988 L.L. Bean, Inc. Courtesy of L.L. Bean, Inc., Freeport, Maine. Used by permission.

This spread is from *Williams-Sonoma Catalog for Cooks – April, 1989.* Courtesy of Williams-Sonoma, San Francisco, California. Used by permission.

From the *Into the Wind 1989 Kite Catalog.* Courtesy of Into the Wind, Boulder, Colorado. Used by permission.

From the *Wireless Late Spring 1989* catalog. Copyright 1989 Minnesota Public Radio. Produced for Minnesota Public Radio by Rivertown Trading Corporation. Courtesy of Minnesota Public Radio. Used by permission.

1992 Printing

Published by NTC Business Books, a division of NTC Publishing Group.
© 1990 by NTC Publishing Group, 4255 West Touhy Avenue,
Lincolnwood (Chicago), Illinois 60646-1975 U.S.A.
Library of Congress Catalog Card Number: 89-60188
Manufactured in the United States of America.

2 3 4 5 6 7 8 9 0 VP 9 8 7 6 5 4 3 2

Contents

Foreword **xi**
Preface **xiii**

————————— CHAPTER ONE —————————

A Catalog Overview

1. Is the Mail-Order Business Really for You?   1

2. Seven Ideas for Successful Catalog Marketing   3

3. The Twelve Most Important Features of Successful Catalogs   4

4. Seven Tested Ways to Put More Oomph into Your Catalog   5

————————— CHAPTER TWO —————————

Making the Most of Creative Concepts

5. The Most Important Catalog Pages   7

6. What the Cover Says about Your Catalog, and Why It's Important   8

7. Your Back Cover Treatment: How Hard Will It Work for You?   11

8. How to Focus Your Customer's Attention on the Product   14

9. Art and Copy Layouts: Which Ones Are Right for You?   15

10. The Differences between Business- and Consumer-oriented Books   18

11. The ABC's of Copy Preparation   20

12. How to Get Your "Thinking Cap" Working on Catalog Copy   21

13. How to Avoid Writer's Block   22

14. Write Seasonal Copy: Your Reward Will Be Higher Response   23

15. How to Write Powerful Captions 23

16. The Magic of Subheads 24

17. The Long and Short of Copy 25

18. How to Write Copy to Fit Small Spaces 26

19. What to Look for in a Catalog Copywriter 26

20. Speaking the Photographer's Language 27

21. How You Select and Pose Models Can Attract or Repel Readers 28

22. Details: If You Can't See Them, You May Not Order the Merchandise 29

23. Your Choice of Type Can Enhance or Confuse Your Catalog 31

24. Ten Ways to Improve Your Order Form 32

25. Keeping Your Identity When Publishing a Sale Catalog 33

26. Minor Alterations to Regular Art and Copy: An Inexpensive Way to Present Sale Merchandise 34

27. Interim Mailings: Is There a Creative Approach That's Right for You? 35

---CHAPTER THREE---

Developing, Choosing, and Testing Effective Lists

28. Establishing a Mailing List 39

29. To Whom Should You Mail? And How Many of Those Names Should Be Rented? 39

30. Where Do You Go to Find Good Lists? 40

31. What You'll Want to Know When Ordering a List 41

32. Why Should You Test Mailing Lists? 42

33. Testing: The Heart of Mail Order 43

34. Regression Analysis Techniques: A Way to Make Compiled Lists More Responsive 44

35. The Whys and Hows of Direct Mail Testing 45

36. How to Select the Number of Names to Test 45

37. List Segmentation Can Improve Response 46

38. Selecting Business-to-Business Lists 47

39. How to Maximize List Rental Income 48

40. Avoid Unwise List Rentals 49

—————————— CHAPTER FOUR ——————————

Choosing and Merchandising Products That Sell

41. That All-Important First Impression: Handling Inquiries for Your Catalog **51**

42. How to Find New Products and New Suppliers without Attending Trade Shows **53**

43. Magazines and Newspapers: A Terrific Resource for New Item Searches **54**

44. Visualization of Art and Copy: A Valuable Exercise When Considering Products for Your Catalog **55**

45. Take Some of the Guesswork Out of Choosing New Items for Your Catalog **56**

46. How to Determine What Your Customer Wants to Buy: Establishing a Customer Preference Guide through Individual Product Sales **57**

47. A Product Information Form: What Is It, and Why Do You Need One? **58**

48. How to Work with Small Suppliers **60**

49. How to Handle Product Suppliers When They Consistently Miss Delivery Dates **61**

50. For a Smooth Operation, Evaluate Your Supplier's Performance at Least Once a Year **62**

51. Drop Shipping: What Is It? **64**

52. Calling Attention to Product Detail: When Does It Pay? **65**

53. Product Education: A Clever Merchandising Approach That Brings in Dollars **66**

54. Tell Your Customer about Your Exclusive Products **67**

55. Arranging Exclusive Listings for Products: The Pluses and Minuses of Seven Different Methods **68**

56. A Celebrity Endorsement Brings Instant Fame to Your Catalog or Product **70**

57. Merchandise Your Credibility: Four Ways to Increase Sales **71**

58. The "Letter from the President": How Important Is It? **73**

59. Don't Overlook Ordering Incentives to Nudge Your Customer into a Purchase **74**

60. The Negative and Positive Aspects of Catalog Sweepstakes Promotions **76**

61. Don't Let the Legal Jargon of Sweepstakes Stop You! **77**

62. Combating the Return Factor while Encouraging the Customer to Order: A Tough Job for the Merchandiser **78**

63. Satisfaction Guaranteed! Words to Live by if You Want Repeat Mail-Order Business **79**

64. How to Price Shipping Charges **80**

65. How to Establish and Register Your Trademark **81**

─────────────────────── CHAPTER FIVE ───────────────────────

Producing and Mailing Your Catalog

66. Where the Money Goes When You're "Buying" Your Catalog 83

67. How to Use Color and Keep Expenses Down 84

68. How Color Separations Are Made 85

69. Computerized Imaging Systems: How They Can Save You Time and Money 86

70. Why Do Beautiful Engraver's Proofs Sometimes Print Poorly? 87

71. How to Get Proper Bids on Your Printing Job 88

72. How to Determine What Kind of Paper You Want 89

73. How to Calculate the Press Run for Your Catalog 91

74. The Benefits of Ink Jet Printing 92

75. How to Choose a Lettershop 93

76. How to Avoid Mailers' Most Frequent Mistakes 94

77. How to Mail—and When to Do It 95

78. Use This Year's Data for Next Year's Decision: When Should You Mail? 96

─────────────────────── CHAPTER SIX ───────────────────────

Marketing Your Catalog to Develop New Customers

79. Prospecting for New Customers with a Mini Catalog 97

80. How to Create a Mail-Order Buyer 98

81. Get a Customer, Not Just a Name! 99

82. Don't Be Afraid to Offer Your Catalog in Space Ads 100

83. How to Decide Which Item to Run in Your Space Ad 100

84. Small Space Ads: Don't Forget the Headline Is the Grabber 101

85. Are There Other Ways to Market Your Catalog? 103

86. More New Fields to Prospect 104

—————————————— CHAPTER SEVEN ——————————————

Telemarketing: Person-to-Person Selling

87. Use This Checklist to Analyze Your Telemarketing Program   105

88. Making the Most of Your 800 Number   106

89. Effective Script Preparation for Telephone Sales   106

90. The "Spike": A Quick-Hitter Promo for the Phone Room   107

91. How to Rate Company Performance by Measuring Incoming Calls   108

92. A "Person-to-Person" Method for Reactivating Customers   109

—————————————— CHAPTER EIGHT ——————————————

Customer Service, Fulfillment, and the Back End

93. Customer Satisfaction: The Bottom Line to a Repeat Mail-Order Business   111

94. How Excellent Telephone Communications Can Give You a Competitive Edge in Customer Service   112

95. Choosing Catalog Software: Inventory Control   113

96. Timely Review of Inventory: The Key to Efficient Stock Control   114

97. Out of Stock, Out of Mind? The Long-Term Impact of Canceling a Customer Order   115

98. How to Write Collection Letters That Work   117

—————————————— CHAPTER NINE ——————————————

Measuring Your Success

99. You Can Turn Catalog Problems into Profit-makers   119

100. Determine and Control Costs: It's the Only Way You'll Target Profits   120

101. How to Analyze a Catalog's Profitability   122

Foreword

The catalog business has been good to Lillian Vernon and especially to me. I like to think that the merchandising principles of Lillian Vernon have been good for the catalog business.

Because of our commitment to this field, we are always pleased when good advice is made available. Maxwell Sroge and the contributors to *101 Tips for More Profitable Catalogs* have made a valuable contribution in gathering this information under one cover.

At Lillian Vernon we firmly believe that our success is based on inspired, talented people paying infinite attention to details. Every customer is special . . . , every order is special . . . , every product is special.

I'm glad *101 Tips for More Profitable Catalogs* takes a similar approach.

Best wishes for your success in the catalog business.

Lillian Vernon Katz
Founder and President
Lillian Vernon Corporation

Preface

Running a profitable catalog is as tough a chore as anybody in any business faces. You have to be a brilliant merchant, a tough-as-nails buyer, and an accounting genius. More than that, you have to be a super judge of creativity, an inspired copywriter, be able to direct tempermental photographers, know all about inventory control and shipping, and, on top of that, have a great eye for graphic reproduction. And that's just the beginning.

101 Tips for More Profitable Catalogs provides a look into what everyday is becoming a more complex business. The "tips" in this book have been contributed by experts, many of whom are considered leaders in their fields of expertise. These top executives generously share their knowledge on such topics as creating the catalog, testing the mailing lists, and choosing and merchandising products that sell.

Consumer and business-to-business catalogs have been one of the great growth industries in America. In my work—consulting with catalog companies and cre-

ating catalogs for them—the difference between winners and losers is almost without exception, the difference between those who respect details and complexities and those who show disdain for the complexities and nuances of the business.

Producing a book like this is no easy chore, especially if you have other significant business responsibilities. Although my name appears on the book, the people who really made it possible, in addition to the contributors, are my good friend and business associate Alice Kimsey who runs Maxwell Sroge Publishing; Ann Keeton, one of the keenest minds I know in analyzing and reporting on business and retailing, who master-minded the organization of the book; and Karen Pochert and Brad Higham who have served so outstandingly as editors of "The Catalog Marketer" newsletter.

Finally, thanks to you for buying this book. May it serve you well.

CHAPTER ONE

A Catalog Overview

WHETHER YOU'RE JUST GETTING STARTED OR YOU'RE already a veteran cataloger, it's a good idea to step back and take a good look at the business.

The following chapter provides a quick overview of what it takes to make a catalog work.

☐

1. Is the Mail-Order Business Really for You?

Many people want to be in mail order, especially after they hear stories of some catalogers' outstanding successes. But is it really that easy?

It's true that, to succeed, you need no special education, no advanced degree and no long apprenticeship. Quite a few successful mail-order specialists started business in something quite different. But observations of successful mail-order people indicate that they share certain characteristics and qualities. Give yourself the following test. You might be reassured about your qualifications—or save yourself some grief. If you plan to work with a mate or partner, answer as a "team." If either one of you has the qualities needed, answer positively. Score 3 points for each question you can answer honestly as "very much," 2

points for those you answer "to a degree," 1 point for "very little," 0 points for "none."

1. Do you have the ability to organize your work and your time? Do you usually accomplish what you set out to do? Are you truly a self-starter, motivating yourself even if nobody supervises you, watches you or cracks the whip? Do you feel you work well on your own, rather than being part of a team or reporting to someone else?

2. Do you stand up well under pressure and frustrations? When things go wrong, can you take it on the chin and bounce back?

3. Do you get along well with people? Though your customer contact will be at a distance, you must have understanding and empathy for people's feelings.

4. Do you have at least an elementary knowledge of ordinary business procedures: filing, typing, bookkeeping, orderly record-keeping?

5. Do you keep abreast of the times through television, magazines, and other media? Do you know what is timely, new, and wanted by the public?

6. Are you the kind of person who generates ideas? Can you look at a procedure objectively, without

thinking "but we've always done it that way"? Can you look at a product or process and think of ways to improve it? Do you see a need for a product or service and wonder "why don't they . . ." or even better, "why don't I?"

7. Do you write well enough to conduct business correspondence with suppliers, customers, business associates?

8. Do you think you have a "nose" for merchandise? Does your personal choice in products, clothing, furniture, etc., usually turn out to be "right"? Do friends compliment you on your taste? Are you usually happy with purchases some time after you've made them?

9. Are you inventive? Can you conceive of or produce any product or service that could be advertised for mail-order sale?

10. Do you have any artistic abilities? Any technical training in art or graphic processes? Can you do paste-up work? Could you prepare illustrations for advertising and catalogs?

11. Can you write copy for catalog promotions and advertising? Do you have slumbering talent you could develop?

12. Do you have a way with figures—a bent for analysis of data? Successful mail order is a numbers game. You must be able to evaluate results or facts, to project costs and profits, to make go/no-go decisions . . . often on the basis of only partial results.

13. Do you have knowledge of business management, or any special aspects of it, such as accounting, control, systems analysis or data processing?

A score of 0 does not destine you for success in the mail-order business. A score of 39 means you're a natural genius and should get started immediately. That leaves those of us in between.

Score 1 to 10. Your chances of success aren't good right now. A high score on at least two of the first three questions indicates you can try to take courses or other instruction to improve yourself in the more "technical" areas.

Score 11 to 20. You're borderline. Again, if you scored well on the first three questions—important because they express your inherent personality traits—you could, with reasonable effort, improve your "score"—your ability to succeed—on points 4, 5, and 7. Proceed with caution. If you feel confident, start to acquire points where you struck out.

Score 21 to 30. Your chances of success are quite good. You probably did well on 1, 2, and 3 and you must have at least three or four areas of technical strength. Exploit your abilities and get competent outside help for those areas in which you need assistance. Take stock, work out your business plans, and take the jump.

Score 31 to 38. You must be a natural; start immediately. Obviously, you have many strengths to build on, many talents to exploit. Work out your business plan with care, because you may be *too* smart, *too* savvy and, therefore, *over*confident. You could be tempted to jump in where others, less talented, might tread more carefully.

Remember, a questionnaire brackets you, but it's far from an accurate tool. You can have a low score and become a roaring success—and you can score in the top 10 percent and lose your shirt. But the person who graduated in the top ten of his medical class is more likely to become a top surgeon than the one who graduated at the bottom, isn't he?

If your score indicates that you lack the personal traits shown in the first three questions, proceed with caution even if your overall score is high. A good manager with strong personal qualities can always hire technicians and specialists. The ability to forge ahead in spite of adversity and to be organized are indispensable traits for success and cannot be hired or bought easily.

Gerardo Joffe, President, Russell's

☐

2. Seven Ideas for Successful Catalog Marketing

Here are some tips to help you plan and launch a successful catalog if you're a beginner, or to keep you on track if you're a seasoned (but possibly jaded) catalog marketer.

1. Don't use tiny type for your catalog and order form copy. Statistical data tell us that about half of the people in the U.S. wear glasses. In a government survey a few years ago it was reported that 11,415,000 Americans have some trouble seeing with one or both eyes—even while wearing glasses. The message is clear: you could easily lose the attention of prospects or customers if they have to struggle to read your 6 point copy.

2. Give advice in your body copy. Sprinkle your catalog copy with advice in the form of side bars that offer tips, techniques, and ideas. When tested, one such catalog pulled almost 50 percent better than a merely product-oriented book. The technique also works with direct mail letters. Renowned agency executive David Ogilvy reported a lift of 75 percent in ad readership when using body copy that gives helpful advice or service. Test the idea.

3. Be specific with your limited-time offers. As a powerful lead and sales stimulator, there's a nothing like a "limited-time offer" to elicit a response from your prospect. But you have a better chance of success if you give a specific cut-off or deadline date. Instead of saying, "Your order must be received within 10 days" say, ". . . by July 1st." As a rule, people need specific rather than general goals. The more specific the offer, the better.

4. Project an image of authority. Create a feeling of authority in your catalog copy. Your objective is to make your program sound like it's the only one of its kind. So pack your copy with authoritative statements and ideas. Testimonials, endorsements, pertinent facts, even statistics can give your presentation an image of authority.

5. Don't be different just to be different. A non-direct response art director creates an offbeat layout to make the ad look different. A copywriter "bends" the copy in a new direction because of weariness with the tried-and-true style the company has always used. A telemarketing rep forgets about proven selling techniques and tries to close a sale in a cute and clever way. And so on. Innovation should be based on tested and proven methods, not on being different just to be different. Just about any direct response or catalog specialist will tell you that you build upon your successes, not upon the trendy, jazzy or unusual situation. To quote the late and great Leo Burnett, "An old boss of mine, the late Homer McKee, once said, 'If you insist on being different just for the sake of being different, you can come downstairs in the morning with a sock in your mouth.'"

6. Write copy promoting benefits. To get more responses or orders, you must push your prospect's "ac-

tion button." Here is an example: If you are selling a man's suit, you can explain the many product advantages of the suit—year-round weight wool, durable cross-stitched buttons and a long-lasting hand-sewn collar and armholes. But selling its ultimate advantages is far more persuasive: the suit makes the customer look smart, handsome, appealing, exclusive, elegant, professional and assured. Plan and develop your copy with the accent on benefits.

7. Show the product in use. This is especially important for new products. If you're selling a weed cutter for the backyard, your photos could show a woman cutting weeds around a tree, a man trimming weeds in a hard-to-reach spot, a woman hanging the cutter up in the garage on its handy storage rack, a man cleaning the cutter with its convenient 3-in-1 cleaning kit and a small child touching the cutter safely because of the cutter's protective casing. Don't just show your reader your product; show it in use. This adds clarity and impact to your story.

Richard Siedlecki, Principal,
Richard Siedlecki Direct Marketing

3.   The Twelve Most Important Features of Successful Catalogs

Catalogs. There are all kinds, but the goal of every single one is *sales*. There are catalogs that sell a general range of merchandise to the consumer, and vertical catalogs that specialize in a single line. Some catalogs sell retail to businesses; others sell wholesale. If these vehicles are geared to mail order, they generate sales directly, and usually immediately. But the scope of catalogs is much broader than mail order alone. Some catalogs support the retail trade by building traffic (a bookstore catalog); some allow a retailer to broaden the inventory he can show to his customers (new car catalogs in dealer showrooms); some promote the product and furnish technical details long after the sales rep has finished his presentation (an IBM catalog on data processing equipment). Some sell a subsidiary product by promoting its use (a Seagram's catalog with food, dessert and liquor recipes); some sell a service as well as a product (a Capp homes catalog); still others sell an idea in order to sell a product (a TWA catalog featuring the delights of London). Almost any product or service can benefit directly or indirectly from a catalog. And every successful catalog has the following features in common:

1. Unified overall appearance

2. Company credibility

3. Logical arrangement of products

4. Clarity of artwork

5. Clear copy description

6. Readability and legibility

7. Product credibility

8. Adequate print job

9. Appropriate technical work

10. Ease of understanding

11. Ease of ordering

12. Satisfaction guaranteed

All of these are up-front incentives to generate the desire to purchase. Successful catalogs have other areas that directly affect the consumer at the back end: prompt fulfillment, quality products, customer service, quality packaging, and so forth. A problem in any of these areas can destroy the long-term effectiveness—sometimes the entire business—of even the most superbly produced creative instrument.

To have a successful catalog, you must carefully consider every one of these features. Though a good catalog seems to be a very simple vehicle, it's easy to see that the scope of features that demand attention is broad and varied. For creative aspects alone you need artists, copywriters, photographers, layout designers, a graphics/production supervisor, and a coordinator who will make sure that art and copy approaches blend with each other and with the overall concept of the catalog. These people must be talented, logical, organized, able to function under deadlines and pressure, and intelligent enough to know when they should check with an expert. These are not simple qualities to find, and they are one of the reasons why people oriented toward the catalog field are becoming more valuable each day.

□

4. Seven Tested Ways to Put More Oomph into Your Catalog

Here are some tried-and-true ways to give your catalog that extra boost by making it inviting and convenient for the customer. Most catalogers are aware of these methods, but that knowledge is not always evident in their finished product. Read this list over, take it to heart and consider whether your catalog could afford to incorporate one, two or all of these points. The difference will show itself in your bottom line.

1. Start selling on the cover. First of all, in three seconds your prospect decides whether to read your catalog or toss it out. You don't want to waste your most valuable time and space with just a pretty picture. (Some catalogs, like L.L. Bean's, do that suc-

cessfully; but their fame lets them get away with it.) Second, showing merchandise on the cover lets your prospect know what you're selling, and it directs them inside.

2. It pays to look good. More attractive layouts increased one cataloger's sales by nearly 20 percent. The improvements included better color photography and color-coded bars running across the top of each page to divide each section.

3. Write a personal letter. Most catalogers know the value of a "Letter from the President" at the beginning of a catalog. But make sure that letter doesn't sound like the "President's Message" in an annual report. It should talk to the reader, give solid reasons to buy, and, like the merchandise on the cover, direct the reader to specific pages.

4. Make it easy to read (I). Stick to simple, clear style. By all means, use poetic devices of mood and feeling to entice the reader. But use simple words and sentences. Complicate a phrase like "To be or not to be . . . ," and you destroy the poetry.

5. Make it easy to read (II). Usually, columns of copy read better than chopped-up blocks. The main thing is not to distract the reader with complicated layouts, hard-to-read, artsy typefaces, or—heaven forbid—reverse type. Every lost reader is a lost sale.

6. Make an offer. You have to start with good merchandise at the right price. But that's not enough. The heart of direct marketing is the *right offer*. Not everyone can afford a sweepstakes, but you can always offer a free gift or bonus for "early bird" orders, or a special discount for large orders. Some catalogers are finding gold in "frequent buyer programs." (One indispensible offer: a solid guarantee. Sears made catalog marketing respectable with an iron-clad guarantee.) Make yours stainless, and your reputation will follow.

7. Put service before sales. The best catalog marketers know ours is a service business. People buy from catalogs for one main reason: convenience. They'll even pay more for the privilege of not having to look for parking, put up with rude sales staff and stand in line.

So you must make it convenient to shop and order from your catalog. That means everything from toll-free, credit card ordering to quick order fulfillment and easy return policies. (One cataloger even offered to pick up unwanted items at no cost to the customer.) Of course, don't offer services you can't afford to provide. Your customers will love you, but they might put you out of business. Just be a friend to customers and they'll return the favor.

Mordechai (Morty) Schiller,
Principal, Schiller Direct Response

CHAPTER TWO

Making the Most of Creative Concepts

THE CREATIVE DEVELOPMENT OF A CATALOG, INCLUD-ing copy, artwork and layouts of pages, gives each catalog its own unique personality. Every detail of your catalog's creative work should fit with the image you want to project.

In this chapter, you'll find some excellent suggestions for making the most of creative concepts.

□

5. The Most Important Catalog Pages

Whether your catalog has 8 pages or 112, some of its pages are simply more visible than others. Whatever you present in these areas will be seen more often than presentations in the rest of the catalog, even by customers who peruse the catalog only briefly.

Basic logic follows: use these highly visible areas to show your strongest items, those most likely to sell well. Not only will they extract a greater volume of sales than they would if placed elsewhere in your book, but they will also be most likely to promise the customer that by viewing the rest of the catalog, he will find other items of interest. Your best items become another "hook" to get the customer to look at your entire catalog.

General Rule: Always put your best items in the most noticeable locations in your catalog. This may be one of the few rules that is identical in retail store setups and mail-order catalogs: give your best items the highest visibility!

In a catalog, the four physical areas that are most prominent are

1. front cover

2. back cover

3. center two pages

4. first two pages inside the front cover

Now that you know the catalog areas you should use to show your best items, how do you decide which items are the best? Obvious and simple? Not when you take a second look.

Whether you have 10 items or 1,000 items in your product line, each can be graded on three scales according to total quantity sold, total dollars grossed, and total profit netted.

The first two scales are often thought of as representative of great items, but the third scale is the only one which really tells you anything about your best items—because it's the bottom line in profit!

Each of these scales is separate and distinct. The items will not fall in the same order in each scale, nor will the order remain the same at different times of the year. Consider the following charts for a leather goods manufacturer during the last quarter of the year.

Total quantity sold		Total dollars grossed			Total dollars netted		
Item	Units	Item	Retail	$ Sold	Item	$ Profit	$ Net
1. Barrettes	5,000	1. Wallet	$ 15	$30,000	1. Clutch	$ 30.00	$15,000
2. Wallet	2,000	2. Portfolio	25	25,000	2. Wallet	7.00	14,000
3. Portfolio	1,000	3. Clutch	50	25,000	3. Portfolio	12.50	12,500
4. Clutch	500	4. Camera Case	70	21,000	4. Suitcase	100.00	10,000
5. Camera Case	300	5. Suitcase	200	20,000	5. Camera Case	30.00	9,000
6. Suitcase	100	6. Barrettes	2	10,000	6. Barrettes	1.50	7,500

If you consider your items "best sellers" only by total quantity sold, you have made an error. While the spread between 5,000 barrettes and 500 clutches is enormous, the dollar gross is reversed. The dollar net in this entire group is even more interesting. The clutch and the portfolio each gross $25,000, but the clutch nets $15,000 and the portfolio only $12,500. In addition, while the wallet grosses more than the clutch or portfolio, it falls in between them in dollars netted.

This situation becomes somewhat more complicated if each of these items has not occupied the identical amount of art and copy space. For instance, if the wallet has received a full page spread in order to net $14,000, but the barrettes have only used one sixth of a page to net $7,500, your decision on which is the better item must additionally be weighted against your page costs and against the fact that the small use of space for the barrettes would allow you to show other profitable items on the same page.

General Rule: When deciding which items to present in your highly visible catalog areas, let economics guide you.

☐

6. What the Cover Says about Your Catalog, and Why It's Important

Front cover graphics for your catalog . . . it's not an easy decision, and too often one of the last re-solved. Before you decide whether to use front cover space to sell your product line, you must decide what you want the graphics to represent about your company, your products, and customers. The cover is the frosting on the cake. Based on its appeal, the customer decides whether or not to open the catalog—a decision so basic that without it you won't sell a thing! With more catalogs competing for the customer's dollar every day, getting the consumer to open and order from your book instead of your competitor's becomes ever more vital.

The style of the front cover gives a myriad of hints to the viewer about what is inside:

- Cost of goods (expensive, middle price range, cheap)

- Category of goods (clothes, gifts, general merchandise, food, stationery, etc.)

- Attitude and image of catalog house (down-home country friendliness, urbane sociability, sweepstake seduction)

- Season to which goods relate (Christmas, autumn, etc.)

- Type of people (customer profile) to which goods are geared (rich/middle-class, country/city, intellectual/physical, refined/simple tastes, business/homebodies)

So much from a cover? Let's examine a few.

The Chris Craft catalog cover in Figure 1 uses its "double C" logo to build the shape of a green Christmas tree against a solid red background. This tells the viewer that it contains products oriented to the

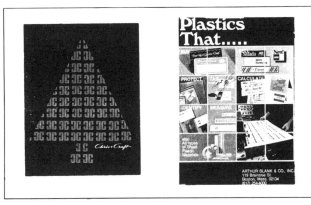

Figure 1

Christmas season; that those products are probably expensive (because of the elegant simplicity of the "designer" logo which creates the tree); and that the catalog house is proud of its image (and consequently reliable) because it chooses to display its logo so prominently. The cover does not tell the viewer what category of goods are inside.

The Arthur Blank & Co., Inc., catalog cover in Figure 1 uses a different technique. It represents the myriad products supplied by the company, and its bold headline tells that they are made of plastic. The products are clearly geared to business rather than consumer trade, implying that the Blank Co. can supply any business need in the plastics area. This cover's one error is the poor readability of the headlines used in the boxes. The headlines try to show the many areas in which the Blank Co. can help fulfill your business needs, but they do not stand out against the back-

ground of the artwork. Consequently, the technique doesn't quite work.

The four covers in Figure 2 tell immediately what category of products are inside, but each projects a different image regarding the cost and style of its contents.

Sporting Life catalog, by its very name, suggests casual and expensive clothes. The pose of the model and the props add to that flavor. The International Boutique suggests more exotic styles. The model's pose and the props in the background imply garments on the costly side. Lane Bryant's busy cover immediately takes it out of the expensive category. This fact is underlined by the slogan "Your dollar buys more at Lane Bryant!" Lana Lobell actually uses the cover to sell a specific item at a very low price. The garment, though on the dressy side, is not designer fashion.

Each of these covers immediately implies the taste, lifestyle and budget of the target customer though the merchandise category is exactly the same. The customer knows what to expect before she even opens the book.

In addition, each of these clothing catalogs presents a cover which is similar in style and mood in every mailing. The customer immediately recognizes the source and each new mailing reinforces the company's image. Figure 3 includes covers that are not explicit about the product line, but do create a distinct company image.

Figure 2

Figure 3

A cover that successfully conveys a distinct image becomes so representative of the catalog company that even from across the room a recipient knows that the new Gander Mountain catalog has arrived. Images like these build customer loyalties by exploiting the comfort of the expected. In addition, images build lists of new customers who are likely to respond to the products being sold in the same way present customers do. This helps create a consistent customer profile while it establishes a company's reputation for a certain type of product.

General Rule: Establish your image and stick with it!

Should Your Front Cover Sell Your Image, or Should It Sell Items, Too?

Do you gain enough having a "hook" to get the customer inside your catalog—having an image with which they are comfortable—or could you gain more by selling from the get-go?

This argument rages among many prominent and experienced catalogers. On one hand, many feel that image is lost or cheapened by using the front cover to pitch items. Others feel that it is insane not to make this space available for sales. (Incidentally, a sales

Figure 4

pitch on a front cover also projects image.) In the middle are those who try to project image and sell items concurrently. These three groups are illustrated in Figure 4.

Of course, there are many variations on each of these themes, all applicable to any product category from gifts to business forms. But just remember, every square inch of your catalog costs you money to pro-duce, . . . and consequently must produce dollars for you. Logic tells us that using cover space to pitch an item is going to bring in more dollars in the long run. How subtle this pitch should be is up to you, and to the image you want to project. If you are just starting your first catalog, try an Image/Sales presentation. The Image-only proponent will tell you that he in-trigues customers into his book with the look of his cover. But without testing alternatives, he'll never know whether or not he really could put this space to better use. And space is expensive!

□

7. Your Back Cover Treatment: How Hard Will It Work for You?

The back cover is the second most visible part of your catalog, and you'd better pay attention to it. Everyone has watched a person walking out of a room and thought, "He can't know what he looks like from that direction, or he wouldn't wear that!" Your rear view makes the second biggest impression about you, and so it goes with the back cover of your catalog. So big an impression that items to which you refer on the back cover will bring you approximately one-third greater sales than if those same items ran in your cata-log without a back cover reference. And items which are placed on the back cover instead of elsewhere in your book will reap appreciably greater sales because of positioning.

General Rule: Don't waste space—it's expensive! Remem-ber that your back cover is one of the most visible areas of your catalog. Use it to represent your image and to make a sales effort as well.

The three most common treatments for back cov-ers are

- to show an item (or items) not shown elsewhere in the catalog, with all information necessary for plac-ing an order (as though the back cover was another page in the book)
- to show items with page numbers referring the cus-tomer elsewhere in the catalog for more complete art and copy information
- to show a company's image (a theme-oriented cov-er, which usually wraps around from the front cover artwork)

These options, some variations, and some strange digressions are shown in Figure 5.

The Neiman-Marcus catalog in Figure 5-A has a strange back cover with no purpose. Nothing is shown but a mailing label block and return address. It truly makes one wonder why. Certainly the blank cover does nothing in the area of image projection, nor in the area of sales. Though NM judiciously guards its classy reputation with understated, aesthetic market-ing techniques, this one is still a puzzle.

The Suburbia, Inc., catalog in Figure 5-B shows an assortment of items carried within the catalog, but doesn't give any page references. Presumably, this cov-er was created to show the vast assortment of items within, a collage effect used to impress and entice. But the execution is poor. The items are not defined clear-ly enough to create a clean, immediately discernable impression, and no page numbers are given to help the possibly enticed customer find the item within the book. This cover couldn't have worked as hard for Suburbia as other options they could have chosen.

The Walter Drake & Sons catalog in Figure 5-C shows specific items with page references to refer the customer inside the catalog for the full pitch. This back cover also takes advantage of space by telling the customer that charge cards are welcomed. In addition, a copy headline tells the customer to look inside for information on an entirely different promotion—the

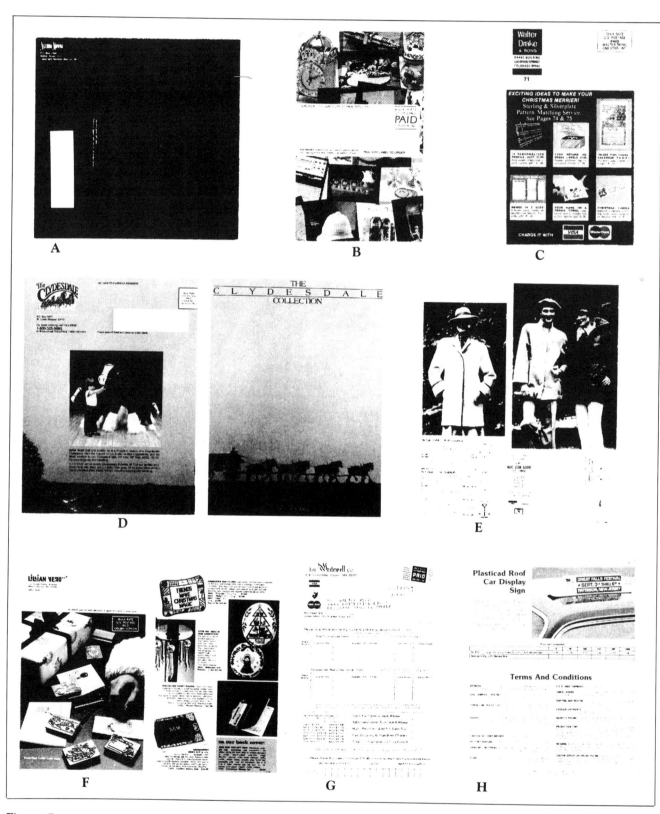

Figure 5

sale of silver flatware. This back cover works hard to take advantage of various marketing benefits, though it does not pretend to offer the class image of either of the preceding examples.

The Clydesdale Collection catalog in Figure 5-D pitches a single item, providing all necessary copy to place an order. This particular catalog used an "image only" front cover, but refused to waste back cover space. There are several questionable areas in the execution of this back-cover sales pitch, however. Basic rules were not accomplished properly: though the black background of the photograph stands out well against the orange cover, the brown stuffed animals for sale do not show up well against it. The copy beneath the photo is a struggle to read, though it tries to send the reader into the catalog for additional sales. One wonders how much better sales might have been if the aesthetics had been accomplished with more clarity.

It's also possible to pitch several items, giving all information needed to close the sale, just as though the cover is a catalog page. Career Guild's clothing catalog, Figure 5-E, is a good example. This technique does not require the duplication of the item elsewhere in the catalog. Additionally, this back cover lets customers know that a toll-free number is available for phone-in orders from charge card holders.

Lillian Vernon, Figure 5-F, refers customers to the inside back cover by picturing the item, but sending the reader inside for the copy pitch. This pulls the customer immediately and easily within the book. This back cover sells an item, but creates an image too. Also, the customer who looks for the ad inside the back cover finds it quickly because of the forethought used by dropping an attention-getting color block behind the copy. Moving inside the book also instantly promotes additional items.

The Writewell Co. catalog, Figure 5-G, uses its back cover to promote its order form. This book does not use a bound-in envelope/order form, as do the others in prior examples. To compensate, the highly visible back cover is used to display the important

form. This decision has severe liabilities. When the customer tears off the order form, the front cover also is lost and the book begins falling apart. An envelope/order form would have given customers a more convenient vehicle for ordering, preserved the condition of the catalog, generated sales with back cover items . . . and more than paid for the order form printing costs!

Another back cover that wastes most of its space is shown in Figure 5-H. The top portion of this Arthur Blank & Co., Inc., catalog pitches an item. But the lower portion displays technical information, much of which is of a negative nature, that could have been placed inside the book. Because this catalog is directed to other businesses, the information is necessary—but more effective sales use should have been made of important back cover space.

In addition to items, other important features to consider for back cover presentation include:

- Charge card logos
- Telephone numbers for phone ordering (especially if toll free)
- "Satisfaction Guaranteed" blurbs
- Credibility blurbs, such as "Serving you well for over 18 years"
- Teasers like "In this issue, special savings on gardening items" or "check page 10 for our special free service"

Because back cover space works hard to increase the sales of items shown on it, be sure you exercise sensible marketing/merchandising judgment in the use of it. Don't present random item choices in this space. Select the most outstanding items in your line. Choose items with two criteria:

- They should be strong sellers. Consider not only the staple items in your line, but also items with seasonal strength, like toys for Christmas, sprinklers for summer, etc.
- They should have excellent profit margins.

After all, if back cover space usage is going to bring you extra profits, you might as well make *maximum* extra profits!

Don't forget to follow the cardinal rule of mail order: always make it easy for your customer to order. The psychology of this rule encompasses the design of your front and back covers, interior layouts, and order form. You can never repeat it too often to your artists and copywriters. Remember it in every element of your catalog, and it will help pay your way to stronger profits.

□

8. How to Focus Your Customer's Attention on the Product

When your customer is visually moving through your catalog, his eyes are moving fast, and his mind is absorbing information rapidly. Anything that is not immediately apparent is either misunderstood or ignored. So although it seems obvious that art and copy are the tools for presenting the product clearly, there are two questions you should ask yourself *after* your product layout is created and *before* it is executed:

- Does this layout leave no doubt as to the product and its function?
- Does this layout make sure that the customer's eye is drawn to the product—and not focused on a less important element?

If you cannot answer both questions with the knowledge that the product has been presented with the strongest focus possible, it's time to go back to the drawing board and start over. If there can be any confusion on the customer's part about these two issues, then your product sales will suffer.

Products with many elements and functions are the most difficult to present simply because the multiple elements can obscure the product's main function. Also, products that resemble something which they are not can fall into the difficult-to-present category, such as an item that looks like a pistol but is really a cigarette lighter. These kinds of products require extra thought in their presentation. Sometimes props can help make the product's function clear—a cigarette and an ashtray might be shown with the pistol lighter, for example. But these decisions are not as clear-cut as they initially seem. Are both the cigarette *and* the ashtray necessary, or would a pack of cigarettes work even better? Which props provide the clearest enhancement and the least distraction to the main focus, the product itself?

When checking your layout against these two questions, it is sometimes handy to have the layout perused by an individual who was not instrumental in its development. Not having been exposed to the concepts upon which the layout was based, this individual will respond to the natural focus of the layout, whereas the artist who created it may be too close to it by now.

Here are two interesting examples to test with our focus questions.

Figure 6-A is from the order form flap accompanying Bloomingdale's Taste of France catalog. Is there any doubt at first glance as to the product? It appears to be Perrier. The headline and the bottle of Perrier are a focal point. When the eye moves to the runners "Perrier" is again seen on the sweatshirts. Sweatshirts? That's the product, in men's, women's and children's sizes. Any confusion caused by this layout could have been quickly eased by changing the headline to "Perrier Sweatshirts."

Figure 6-B, from Wine Ambience Catalog's order form flap, focuses attention so strongly on the reversed-out headline at the top that one's first impression is that this ad is for *The Wall Street Journal*. The advertising philosophy of "status by association" tries to put the *Wine Spectator* in the same class as a presti-

Figure 6-A

Figure 6-B

gious, authoritative newspaper—a very good idea—but misses the mark by seeming to promote the wrong product first. The viewer's first instinct is to say, "How strange! What's an ad for *The Wall Street Journal* doing in this catalog?" What could have been done to alter this impression and shift the focus to the proper product? Perhaps if the point size of the type used for *The Wall Street Journal* copy was smaller than the point size used for the *Wine Spectator* copy, the emphasis could have been shifted toward the appropriate item. Or if the two copy areas had not been split, the viewer's eye wouldn't have had to drop to the bottom half of the ad before it got the point—especially since the "weight" is at the top of this ad, without much left to pull the eye down. This is a typical back-to-the-drawing-board situation, because several options exist for dealing with the problem, and these options must be worked on visually to determine the best solution.

Tuck the focal point questions in the back of your mind and pull them out to use during your next creative session. Perhaps they'll help.

☐

9. Art and Copy Layouts: Which Ones Are Right for You?

One of the great excitements about catalog marketing is the ready availability of your competitors' books for perusal and study. The successes and failures of the catalog marketplace make themselves apparent at every turn. All you have to do is watch and analyze! Giving competition the eagle eye is as easy as trotting to your mail box and examining carefully the catalogs you receive. This is of the greatest value when you record the information you accumulate, and continue to record it precisely and analytically.

General Rule: Watch, record, study, learn, improve. Don't forget these five steps to knowing your competition, and you'll have a vehicle for your own growth and strength.

One area you can examine easily is the art and copy page layouts of other catalogers. Every catalog has photographs and copy on each page, but there are a million approaches to putting them together. Decisions must be made continually:

- How many items should you show on a page?
- How much space should be devoted to art, and how much to copy?
- Should the placement be symmetrical or asymmetrical?
- Should the photos vary in size or be the same?
- Should your art be in color or black and white? (Some items can be presented more clearly with black and white art.)
- Should the photos bleed off the page, or be bordered?
- Should the items in the photos be fully enclosed by the art block, or should they bleed out of it?
- Should the background on some items be completely dropped out?
- Should several items be shown in a single large photo, or should each item have an individual presentation?
- What type face should be chosen for the copy?
- How large should the type's point size be?
- Should the type be black? Should it be printed against a white background?
- Should the copy be printed flush left and right (each line justified to the same width) or ragged?

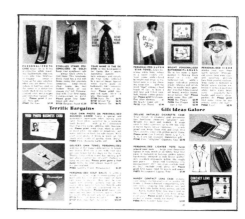

Figure 7

Figure 8

Let's examine some variations. Figure 7 (Walter Drake & Sons, Inc.) shows the most traditional, symmetrical layout we could find. The copy and art share almost an identical amount of space each. The pages are equally balanced. Each copy block prints every line an identical width.

Advantages: It's easy for the customer to see which artwork matches which copy block. The eye is never confused. All items share equal prominence. Copy size and type style are very readable; black type against white background has the greatest clarity. Items can be easily interchanged throughout the book because of equality of space allotment.

Disadvantages: Without careful variation of other page layouts throughout the book, this style could

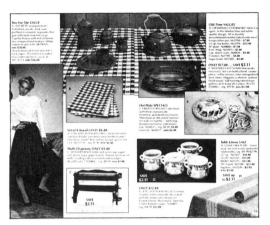

Figure 9

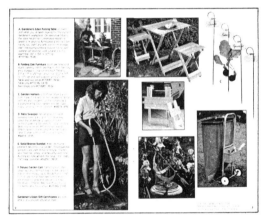

Figure 10

become static, boring. The lack of easy variation to the size of copy and art space could hurt items needing more space for freer, optimum presentations. Innovations in layout must be kept to a minimum, for they would stick out like a sore thumb in layouts of this "locked-in" style.

The Spencer Gifts Catalog in Figure 8 has been chosen to show how a layout similar to the one mentioned above appears after certain alterations. This layout is not as crisp, mainly because the photos bleed off the page; they are not framed in between with as much "air," and consequently have a tendency to run into each other. The type size is smaller and the headlines on each copy block are not as bold. The black

type at lower left and right is against a colored background, making it somewhat less readable than against a white background.

Advantages: The photos are larger than those in Figure 7, allowing the items to be larger (and presumably more easily seen). But the sacrifice of "air" around each photo makes them lose individual snap.

Disadvantages: Though the layout strives for a less symmetrical, more interesting look than Figure 7, it is somewhat cluttered and its "tightness" is not relaxing and pleasant to the eye. Notice, too, that this catalog shows nine items on the two pages, while Figure 7 shows twelve.

New Hampton's catalog (Figure 9) displays an asymmetrical layout where a lot of good judgment has been exercised. The areas occupied by art and copy are well balanced within the format, avoiding the choppy look from which a layout like this so frequently suffers. The type is large and readable, though the combination of upper and lower case in the headlines is a bit confusing to the eye. They don't stand out with the clarity a headline should offer.

Advantages: This style of layout is never boring. Each item asks for attention in turn.

Disadvantages: It's easy to get chaotic with a free layout; there's always the risk that the viewer may not be able to match copy and art to each other instantly.

Gardener's Eden (Figure 10) handles the problem differently. The art is placed together, and so is the copy. The customer must reference the letter in the photo to the letter introducing each piece of copy. Each double-page spread presents six or seven items, less than the other books. But clarity is maintained, the copy is nicely spaced, and the headlines stand out.

Advantages: The appearance presented to the customer is neat, clean, simple. There is no difficulty in finding the copy that elaborates on the photo, as long as the letters can be easily found in each photo. Obviously this is of major importance.

Disadvantages: The photos must do most of the work. Because the copy is not immediately available to assist the customer, he must look elsewhere for it,

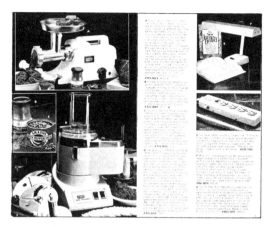

Figure 11

Figure 12

lack of white space and the poor positioning and balance of photos and copy.

___

General Rule: Always make it easy to match the copy with the art, no matter what style of layout you choose.

___

□

___

10. The Differences between Business- and Consumer-oriented Books

The differences between business- and consumer-oriented books are a matter of the catalog's philosophy toward the buyer's psychology. It's an old story: it doesn't matter what you're selling; what matters is to whom you're selling it. And the success of that sale depends on how well you match your selling technique to your target market.

Let's work backward from a single area of observation to draw some conclusions. One large difference between most business-to-business catalogs and most catalogs oriented toward the individual consumer is the way items which compete against each other are positioned. Business-geared books group the competing items; consumer-geared books spread competing items throughout. There are a few assumptions made about the philosophy and psychology of the customers reading the catalogs which cause those opposite creative approaches.

There is some crossing of these philosophical lines, but usually only when the consumer-directed book sells a single category of product, such as stationery and greeting cards. But even then, it would be unusual to see all of the birthday cards juxtaposed. More likely one would see a group of birthday cards (perhaps comic in nature) on page 3, another group

meaning that the photo must intrigue the customer enough to justify this effort.

Williams-Sonoma (Figure 11) uses a similar layout. The copy is also in a column, not placed immediately beside the item. But the lack of bold headlines or spacing to gap and separate each piece of copy and art makes it seem awesome and difficult to read.

Duncraft (Figure 12) uses large art to show only about six items per double-page spread. The catalog uses no white backgrounds anywhere in the book, putting the copy to severe disadvantage because it is hard to read. Though the pages are not crowded with items, the book borders on cluttered because of the

Business Catalog

1. The customer's *need* outweighs the customer's desire.

2. The no-time-to-waste business person must be able to *find areas of specific interest* immediately.

3. Because of need, the customer must buy anyway. So the problem becomes dealing with competition from other catalogs, rather than *competing items*.

Consumer Catalog

1. The customer may have a need, but it is outweighed by *desire.*

2. The browsing consumer must be encouraged (forced?) to *peruse all areas of the catalog,* with the hope that many desires will be met along the way.

3. Because desire is assumed to outweigh need, the problem is to enhance *individual items* by downplaying competing items.

(sentimental florals) on page 20 and a further group (photographs of people) on page 40. The idea still is to keep the customer turning pages to find more birthday cards while viewing anniversary cards and notepaper along the way.

Various techniques are used in business-to-business books to make finding categories simpler. Anything that makes it easier for your customer to arrive at the moment of placing the order is an enhancement to your catalog. So, though a business-oriented catalog makes it easy for its customers to find all of the adding machines, a consumer-oriented catalog might borrow some of these techniques to allow its customers to locate easily all of the kitchen items. Even though a consumer-oriented catalog may not wish to place three styles of graters on the same page, it often wishes to categorize *related* items (a cheese grater, carrot curler and radish rosebudder). This way, products with identical functions may not be placed right next to each other, but instead products with *related* functions are. This makes things easy for the consumer and encourages extra sales of related items.

These examples from the DLM (Developmental Learning Materials) catalog show an interesting concept used to help customers locate areas of interest. Figure 13 is the first page of the catalog, and it's devoted to a table of contents. Each band features a different category and is printed in a different color. Inside the catalog, the same band runs across the top of the pages which match each category (see Figure 14). A customer can flip through the pages and easily locate the color-keyed category.

Figure 13

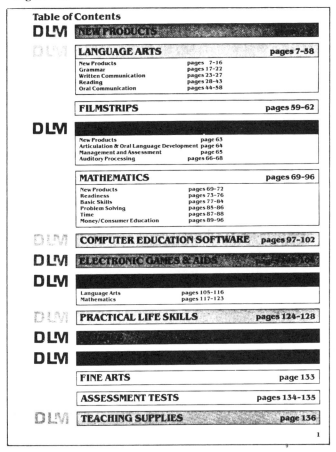

Figure 14

of the Brood Mare
Foal

atic photographs taken during
ual birth show students all the
details of care before and after
g that are necessary for healthy
ng and the mare's safety.

Filmstrip
-133) **$35.00**

The Western Equitation
Class

Show your students how to mount,
dismount, achieve the proper seat,
hand positions, back the horse and
much much more to help them score
higher in contests!

Sound Filmstrip
(1-461-135) **$35.00**

lish Equitation

omprehensive filmstrip
nstrates the basics of riding for-
in the seat to riding at the hand
and jumping. A special
nce on leads, photographed
high-speed camera, shows
hey apply to the canter.

Filmstrip
-134) **$35.00**

Hoof Care

Help your students understand foot
anatomy and the functions of each
part of the hoof with this step-by-step
approach for trimming or repairing
hooves to their proper conformation.

Sound Filmstrip
(1-461-136) **$35.00**

ANIMAL SCIENCE

ORSEMANSHIP KIT

Help Students Get The
Most From Their Animals!

Figure 15

The final eight pages of this catalog are indexes: alphabetical by product, alphabetical by subject and numerical by product code number. There is no reason for the first-time or reorder customer to have any difficulty ordering from this product line.

A consumer-oriented catalog could easily borrow the same techniques (with the exception of the final indexes, which really would be unnecessary) to aid the customer while adding graphic appeal to the book. Categories could be Kitchen Helpers, Bath and Personal Accessories, Home Decorating Aids, Stationery Items, Christmas Gifts under $25, etc.

The Vocational Education Productions (California Polytechnic State University) catalog also groups categories, but the method they use to flag this idea is vague to the viewer. Figure 15 is the upper right quarter of a page, and shows the method they use: the category is printed sideways in the upper corner. It is difficult to read, not instantly apparent, and the type style is a little too busy. The triple silhouette of the animal adds to the eyes' confusion. If you add something to your catalog which is intended to make things simpler for the customer, it should not merely clutter

the page; it should be a *functional* addition. No matter how good the idea, discard it if you cannot incorporate it effectively—or keep trying until you can. If you cannot make the idea work, you end up hindering the layout.

Though there are some style differences between business-to-business catalogs and individual consumer-oriented catalogs, these differences are occasioned by one of the basic rules of mail-order design: simplicity and ease. Once you have honed in on your customer's style of purchasing, use whatever techniques are necessary to make it easy for the customer to find—and order—what he's looking for.

☐

11. The ABC's of Copy Preparation

Artwork attracts, enhances and creates desire; but *copy sells*. Far too many managers are mostly concerned with how their products look, what colors will be used and how beautiful the catalog will be. They often treat copy and the copywriter's role as secondary. This is a big mistake! Management must learn, understand and accept the fact that the copywriter should be involved in every aspect of catalog creation, development and production, from initial product selection meetings to final blueprints and color keys. The copywriter's job is to thoroughly study the company, its audience and product line before promoting the individual items in the catalog. That study should include the following steps:

1. List evaluation and analysis. Simply put, you cannot write selling copy unless you know to whom you are writing.

2. Overall product selection. The writer must understand why each product (or service) has been

selected for a specific issue of the catalog. What's more, the writer should have a voice in suggesting changes in product selection, especially if he or she feels that including certain products can destroy an overall "feel" or uniqueness for the catalog. At the very least, the writer should know why each product fits in the line being promoted.

3. Audience history. A writer approaches lists of customers differently than prospects; and he or she tackles different prospect lists differently. It is important for management to make all "audience facts" known to the writer at the outset.

4. Investigation. Give all products and all accessories to the writer. Don't forget to include support literature and documentation on how the product was developed or manufactured. Allow time for your writer to get the feel of each item and to feel good about each one. He or she will write better than if you simply provide photos.

5. Field time. Your writer should be able to test your products and see how they are used by the very people to whom they are to be sold. The same applies to selling services in a catalog. Bring your writer into focus groups to listen and ask questions. Let him or her examine your contracts and policies and go with your service people to a few actual jobs. Let your writer go on sales calls to gauge customer and prospect reactions and learn new product benefits.

6. Question time. Before and during writing, your writer must be able to question you, your engineers, merchandisers, customers and salespeople. Deny these opportunities at your peril!

7. Thinking time. The good copywriter doesn't just start writing. A writer thinks, sometimes for a long time, before turning on a typewriter. Copy will flow beautifully and be more successful if he or she has had a chance to structure it mentally first.

You stand the best chance of motivating your prospects to buy with believable copy, frank state-

ments of value and a strong sales pitch. And that can only come from a writer who has spent ample time with you and your products.

René Gnam, President, René Gnam Consultation Corporation

12. How to Get Your "Thinking Cap" Working on Catalog Copy

There are no basic rules, but there are some easy procedures that may assist you in starting the thinking process!

Clean your desk. Unclutter it. Take out a pad or scratch paper and a pen or pencil—not a typewriter. Longhand allows you to think longer: your mind rests a bit instead of speeding along with typewriter keys in an attempt to make a deadline or churn out the copy. So answer these questions in longhand on your pad:

- Who is my target audience?
- Why will this product or idea appeal to them?
- What benefits does the product, idea or service provide to the audience? (Write down every single detail you can think of.)
- How does my product beat the competition?
- What is special about my offer and how can I rework it into a dramatic mind-catcher?

Perhaps all this appears a bit simplistic on the surface. But these procedures will not only get you started writing about the product, they'll also help you go about writing it from a fresh point of view.

The trick to making this procedure work is really concealed in the third point. When you're writing down every detail, you should actually *overwrite*. Besides being easier to cut than to add, this method helps you overcome writer's block. Don't think about how many lines you have to write; don't think about the order in which you should make your points; don't think about whether you're expressing yourself effectively or not. Just write. Writer's block is usually caused because you're trying to edit at the same time you're trying to write. The scientific editing part of your brain inhibits the creative part from expressing itself.

Like every direct marketer with an open mind, you're always looking for new ways to think. So try answering these simple questions next time you're stumped by a copy problem. They'll trigger you to use the talents you often can't put to work because the deadline or the "sameness" of the product or marketing objective prevents your mind from getting to work.

Here are two everyday phrases you can refresh with this method. As you review them, think about how you can come up with your own ways of saying the same thing. Instead of "call toll free, 1-800-777-0000," try "for immediate action, call toll free, etc." Instead of using an order form and adding your toll-free number somewhere in your catalog copy, try adding a tag line in fairly large type at the bottom of the order form: "For faster-than-mail action, call 1-800-777-0000."

René Gnam, President, René Gnam Consultation Corporation

☐

13. How to Avoid Writer's Block

Copywriters who have no trouble dishing up a sales letter or ad suddenly freeze when faced with the task of producing 180 lines of 44 characters each for a collection of items in a catalog. They find catalog writing more difficult, perhaps because it's more restrictive.

In an ad or sales letter, the writer is pretty free to let loose. But in a catalog the writer is limited in space and confined to following the catalog's set tone, format and style. Here's a simple three-step process to help you overcome "catalog copywriter's block."

1. In the first stage, simply ignore the constraints of space, format, and style—just write. Let the words flow. Write whatever comes naturally. Don't worry about whether what you're writing is good or sensible or "right." You'll have a chance to go back and fix it later. Right now, just let the words pour out.

Some writers like to keep two pads in front of them as they write. The first pad is used for composing the copy. On the second, they jot down any stray thoughts or phrases that come to mind, but don't fit in with the copy, for future reference.

2. In the second stage, edit your rough first draft to make it better. Editing consists of the following:

- Deleting unnecessary words and phrases
- Adjusting the copy to the exact word length the specs call for
- Rewriting awkward phrases
- Making sure all necessary facts appear
- Rewriting to fit the catalog "tone"
- Reordering copy points to make the organization more logical
- Making copy conform to catalog format and style (adding tables, charts or special sections, as needed)

3. The third step is polishing. Polishing means proofreading, checking for errors in spelling, punctuation, grammar, capitalization, abbreviation. It also involves checking details like product numbers, product specifications, registration and trademarks, and technical accuracy.

Every writer has a "creative" side and an "analytical" or "editing" side. The creative side comes up with ideas; the editing side holds them up to the cold light of day and judges their effectiveness. Both are needed in copywriting, but should be used in separate and distinct phases of the writing process. When you try to be creative and analytical at the same time, your editing faculties inhibit your creative juices . . . that's one form of "writer's block."

Robert W. Bly, Copywriter/Consultant

☐

14. Write Seasonal Copy: Your Reward Will Be Higher Response

The writer who fine-tunes copy for seasonal impact is a savvy direct marketer. Seasonal catalogs—Easter, Winter, Christmas, etc.—must be prepared several months in advance in order to be issued at least six weeks before the holiday or season arrives, with eight weeks being preferable. It's not unusual for a first drop to occur even twelve or more weeks prior to a major holiday, like Christmas.

But when should you write such catalog copy? The most appropriate time is during the season itself. Thus, if you are creating next year's Christmas catalog, write it during this Christmas season; that's when you are in a festive holiday mood. That joyous attitude will be evidenced in your copy, enabling you to relate much better in the following year.

To meet production deadlines, many marketers are forced to prepare Christmas catalog copy in June and July. Then their mental attitude is oriented toward outdoor activities and sunshine—precisely the wrong atmosphere for preparing Christmas copy.

The same thing holds true in quarterly catalogs. Try to do next year's spring catalog while this year's forsythia is in bloom. Don't do it in the fall when the weather is turning chilly. Some writers are able to practice this ideal. Others create a setting most nearly

matching the season about which they are writing by traveling to an appropriate locale with a portable typewriter.

But the key is to get a seasonal flavor in your main headlines, your theme photography and your product descriptions. You'll sell more down jackets if you can include a seasonal impression of winter hiking in the description of your item.

You can start toward next year's catalog right now. If it's spring, write some tag lines and theme copy for next spring's catalog. Sit down with your old spring catalog and rewrite copy for next year . . . on the best movers, of course.

☐

15. How to Write Powerful Captions

Various studies have indicated that captions are the best-read type in any publication, including catalogs. Thus, whenever possible, include at least one caption with a photo, because the caption draws the eye from the photo to the descriptive product copy.

Here are the most prominent guidelines for catalog caption writing:

1. *Benefits.* Include one or more major user benefits in your captions to entice readership of the main copy block.

2. *Features.* Product features, such as the number of knobs on a radio, can be very short inset captions, if you have space limitations.

3. *Marriage.* You get benefits from features, so marry those two points. Example: "This rotating antenna lets you clearly tune in distant stations."

4. *Involvement.* Instead of merely stating a benefit, tell why it's important from a "use" point of view. Example: "You'll slice every tomato easier with the extra-sharp blade."

5. *Future tense.* Promising the reader how he will benefit in the future creates a strong desire for ownership.

6. *Terseness.* Make captions lean. Each word counts. Your reader has looked at the photo and may be only cursorily interested. Involve him with a tightly-written enticement.

7. *Length.* Tight writing does not mean you must write "short." Long, benefit-laden captions can work well.

8. *Multiple captions.* The more captions you use, the more action perceived for the photo and the more uses perceived for your merchandise. Use multiple captions when possible, but cite different copy points in each.

9. *Facts.* Readers expect in captions facts which will involve them, not flowery phrases. Facts are strong convincers. Flowers detract.

René Gnam, President, René Gnam Consultation Corporation

☐

16. The Magic of Subheads

Many products merit lengthy catalog descriptions to involve the reader. But lengthy copy can appear boring if it's simply a mass of type of constant width and size.

One way to "open up" long copy blocks is to use ragged right type instead of justified (making all lines exactly the same length). Other ways include using bold face or italic type, and lead-in lines, indented first lines in paragraphs, a bit of extra spacing between lines and/or paragraphs, and bulleted or asterisked benefits or lists of features.

One of the best methods to make copy displays appear airy is to use subheads—two- to five-line headings inserted between paragraphs. Ideally, two paragraphs should follow each subhead.

Subheads can

- be numbered in reading sequence
- tell a complete story
- command continued readership
- command a response
- point out benefits in the copy that follows (This is the most common usage and should be combined with the previous point for greater motivation.)

Subheads should not be

- mysterious or unclear
- unfathomable when read separately
- bland statements of what follows
- used so often that you seem to have a mass of small, screaming headlines
- labels, like "Product Features"

Subheads should

- break up long columns of type
- guide a skim-and-scan reader to sections of greatest interest
- communicate reader benefits
- introduce important concepts
- be the same color as body copy

This last "should" is particularly important. Just because you have a full-color catalog doesn't mean you have to use a ton of color for subheads. Subheads are *part* of body copy. As a device to get readers into that copy they should be printed in the same color. Yes, there are exceptions; mainly for stress. But the general guideline is use subheads to serve scanning readers, letting them pick copy blocks *they* want to read, and then getting them right into the copy.

Scanning readers toss your catalog if subheads fail to convince them to read your copy. Be sure to write your subheads so your readers are "gripped" to read the copy that follows.

René Gnam, President, René Gnam Consultation Corporation

□

17. The Long and Short of Copy

The old saying "copy should be just as long as necessary" often is misinterpreted. Some people believe copy should be stripped to the bare bones, containing just a few exciting words to make your mouth water and that's it. But your copy needs a lot more.

Here are the absolute essentials. There must be a headline or a lead-in sentence. Its purpose is to attract attention and encourage the reader to read on for more information. The next sentence or sentences need to outline the facts. The writer must outguess the reader and counter all objections with a positive answer. Every statement should encourage the reader to say, "Yes, I want this one." And when he reads the last word, he should have been told everything needed to make a buying decision. This would include size, weight, colors, what it's made of, etc. Naturally, your designer and photographer can often help by incorporating a lot of facts into the photo. Between copy and photo, every conceivable question must be answered.

Sometimes all of this can be accomplished in just a few words. Some excellent copy does a marvelous selling job and takes up less than three lines of type. But often this is not the case. Some products—especially complex products—may require a great deal more explaining, and their copy should be long. Designers may not like long copy and often will create a catalog with too little space. Copywriters and artists can resort to some unbelievable quarrels. If it comes to that, then the copywriter must take over and rule the roost. Photographs and design can't always answer all the questions and get the story across.

Whether it is short or long, copy must also sing. The reader must enjoy reading and automatically read on. This should be the case even if the copy is a mere three lines long. Write in short sentences and your copy often sings automatically.

Don't write long copy just to write long copy. If three lines is all you need, then write three lines. Don't lose your buyer by including a lot of unnecessary garbage. Below are two pieces of copy on the same product.

COPY A:

BRIGHT, CLOSE-UP VIEWS WITH THE ILLUMINATING 30X MAGNIFIER. This convenient pocket magnifier is designed to be a valued companion for work, hobby or recreation. Its diminutive size ($5\frac{1}{2}'' \times 1\frac{3}{4}''$) allows it to slip easily into pocket or purse; its 30X makes it ideal for detailed examination of plants, gems, stamps, photos. It features a center focus wheel for precise one-hand operation; retractable condenser lens pinpoints light so you can zero in on your subject. Light source is built-in; batteries not included. A really handy tool.

30X MAGNIFIER NO. 3291 $12.95

COPY B:

ILLUMINATING 30X MAGNIFIER IS POCKET-SIZED. Ideal for a detailed inspection of plants, gems, stamps or photos. It features a center focus wheel for precise one-hand operation, a retractable condenser lens to pinpoint light and a built-in light source. Batteries not included. $5\frac{1}{2}'' \times 1\frac{3}{4}''$.

30X MAGNIFIER NO. 3291 $12.95

The short copy "B" says everything necessary. Copy "A" is packed with unnecessary words. Notice how the headline for "B" immediately gets the message across and saves at least twelve words.

☐

18. How to Write Copy to Fit Small Spaces

Start this exceptionally difficult job with this approach: *before writing,* review the major descriptive points and benefits. Then write the copy as long as it needs to be to cover everything. Tighten it. Rewrite it. This is the time to start enforcing discipline:

1. Speak to the artist to determine which type styles will be used, in what size, for what width and how many lines.

2. Speak to the typesetter to determine the character count per line. (If you're familiar with copy casting, you can do this yourself after your artist has indicated fonts, sizes and widths).

3. Set typewriter margins to the character count per line.

4. Rewrite the copy to fit the new margins. In doing this you constantly will be frustrated by the narrow margins, but they will lead you to find shorter, crisper words. Those short margins force you to edit your copy to be truly lean.

The artist and writer should work together to achieve the desired "look" and selling messages. After the writer has gone through these editing steps, layout revisions may be required so that copy will not be shortchanged. And each time layouts are revised, the writer must re-edit or rewrite.

René Gnam, President, René Gnam Consultation Corporation

☐

19. What to Look for in a Catalog Copywriter

Just as ownership of a camera does not make one a photographer, writing ability alone does not make a copywriter—especially a catalog copywriter. Yet, every week new resumes hit the desk, extolling the applicant's academic credentials, listing courses in advertising, perhaps even including some previous job experience as a "copywriter."

Sadly, when put to the test of writing real-life catalog copy, most of these applicants will not measure up. Yes, they write smoothly; yes, they string words together easily; yes, they really do "love to write." But their copy fails to translate into orders.

Why? Simply because they mistakenly believe that writing skill is the name of the game. The fact is, *selling* is the required experience. A good salesperson with even modest writing ability will always outperform a good writer, period. What should you look for in a writer's background?

1. Your applicant should have had face-to-face contact selling to customers over a period of time. This could be in part-time work while attending school. It could be over-the-counter retail in a department store, the local pharmacy, even a fish market. My favorite is "direct selling," once called door to door. One powerful catalog copywriter earned his wings as a radio announcer, ad-libbing around mediocre commercial copy in order to make the spots pay off. Switching to salesmanship in writing was a natural progression.

2. He or she should have acquired personal experience in overcoming sales resistance through give and take. The Britannica salesman and the Avon lady know what we mean. "My husband's not home and I have to get his okay first." "I can't afford it now." "I don't like the color . . . the style . . . the warranty. . . ." A salesperson who can be turned away by the first objection soon will be in some other line of work.

With only quickness of wit and persuasiveness of pen, the effective catalog copywriter anticipates what a potential customer might want to know, what the objections to buying might be, and addresses them.

3. The catalog copywriter should be, above all, a mail-order copywriter. The task of selling in a catalog is accomplished through words and pictures. There, often in space too restricted for conventionally long mail-order exposition, the skillful copywriter must punch home the complete message. G.K. Chesterton once apologized for a lengthy letter to a friend by noting that he "hadn't the time to write a short letter."

In this effort, a personal selling background is far more important to your catalog than mere cleverness, dazzling "wordsmithing" or even commendable scholastic achievement. Mail-order copy is not supposed to be pretty; it's supposed to work.

However, remember that it's not necessary to give up on writing that also reads well and respects the language. Good *selling* copy *can* be produced which also maintains a distinctive communicative style for your catalog.

Jack Schrier, President, The Copy Shoppe

20. Speaking the Photographer's Language

Though red is red and blue is blue, many people's answers will vary slightly when asked what color they see. When subjective judgment is involved, no answer may be entirely correct. There are common terms from the graphics world used daily by photographers, printers, separators and catalogers that have different meanings to each. An unawareness of these differences can result in costly mistakes. Knowing the definitions attached to these terms helps your catalog move along smoothly as you communicate on com-

mon ground—and this is sure to pay off somewhere along the production cycle.

Chrome. To the photographer it's an abbreviation of Ektachrome, Kodachrome or any other transparency film. A separator or printer uses the word as a shortened version of the trade name "Chromalin," a proof system by DuPont. Chrome is sometimes misused to designate any color proof made from separation films.

Negatives. A photographer considers this the film in his camera which eventually produces color prints or black and white prints. To the separator and printer, the word designates the film material used to represent the separate colors in a four-color separation of original photographs or art—each negative corresponding to magenta, cyan, yellow and black.

Positives. This represents the end result of the image the photographer has taken, whether a black and white or color print, transparency or video. The separator or printer calls the contact film made from separation negatives and used for final plate making the "positives."

Art. Confusion is caused by this relatively innocent term. To the photographer, art is anything drawn, not photographed. The separator and printer group *all* illustrations, including photography (sometimes even pasted up type), and call them original art.

Focus. Critical to the photographer, focus defines the sharpness of his photograph. In the terminology of the separator and printer, focus delineates the percentage scale of the original to the final image reproduced in print; i.e., focus at 50 percent (half size).

Copy. A photographer or art studio uses this word to represent the short lines or paragraphs that describe the merchandise. But the people dealing with ink lump together the artwork, photography, and words that are to be printed and call all of them copy.

To confuse the situation even more, there are common meanings in the industry that are attached to totally different words. Often you'll find that the region of the country dictates which term is used. For example, Silhouette, Outline, C.O.B. (Crop Out Background) and Dropout all mean an image to be printed without a background. Keyline, Pasteup, Mechanical, Boards, Mechs, and Camera-readies all mean a black and white art board to show the separator and printer exact placement of all elements (art, photos, type).

Other terms fall in these same areas of confusion, so be alert to the possibility that almost any term can be misunderstood. One thing is clear: to get the best possible results from your photographer, your separator and your printer, define your terms. Even if you think you understand the meaning of the words they're using, *ask*. You'll save money and frustration.

James A. Semsar, The Studio

□

21. How You Select and Pose Models Can Attract or Repel Readers

When the copywriter plans a catalog, or an individual product segment, he must visualize the display simultaneously with creating the selling words. If he doesn't he can't sell with maximum effectiveness. So the successful promotion writer examines all mailing list data before turning on the typewriter. Then he's sure that benefit and description copy is targeted to the names on the lists being used . . . and this becomes a guide on how to cue the artist and photographer.

Here are general guidelines on selecting models and posing them, so that the first time your reader spots a photo, he immediately identifies himself and thus can relate to the product being merchandised:

1. Age. This is critical. Do not use a teen-ager if list research shows you'll be mailing to senior citizens. Because readers identify with those who are closest to themselves, you want someone within the age bracket of the list audience. And because younger readers subconsciously respect those who are a touch older than themselves, you want a model in the upper third of your list audience. So . . . select a model whose age is in the upper one-third of the age range of the bulk of your prospects. If the lists you use constitute 25–40 year olds, your model should be 35–40.

2. Sex. Starch studies show males are not attracted primarily to females, but females are attracted primarily to other women. So, do not write copy or select models based on the opposite sex. Instead, select the sex matching that of the greatest number of names on your lists: and if your lists have a 50/50 sex split, try using one male and one female model.

3. Product identity. Write copy and select models for the prime users of specific products. Your reader knows that a safety relief valve on an industrial boiler is not operated by a woman and that, unless you mail to tailors, presser feet on sewing machines are not used by men.

4. Product ease. Often it pays to use more than one photo to demonstrate equal product appropriateness for males and females and to visually communicate that both sexes can easily use your item.

5. Seemliness. The hunk who runs your farm tractor should not look like a corporate chairman. But if it's a suburban lawn tractor, that's different. Readers should instantly see that models are fit for the product's use.

6. Expression. People shudder at traumas, crises, unpleasant situations. The model in your two-piece bikini should look like she's enjoying herself. Many apparel promoters mistakenly pose models to look as if they're in extreme pain. Would you want to buy a bathing suit that gives you such discomfort? Remember, you are not selling a garment or equipment. You're selling its enjoyment, utility, status, convenience . . . its glow.

7. Use applications. Show the model exulting over possession of your product (perhaps smiling as she serves the meal she prepared with your cookware). But just show her hands as she fills the pots and places the pans on the stove. That way the reader sees the glow and recognizes the utility. (Often you will want to select a different model for hand shots).

8. Involvement. Products displayed by themselves create less desire for ownership than products displayed with someone using them, enjoying them, benefiting from them. But that does not preclude also showing your product separately, perhaps from several views, so the reader sees the full scope of your merchandise.

9. Site. Let the customer visualize wearing his tux at La Scala. And remember, a compresser does not belong in a showroom. Show the customer how easy it is to hook up in his workshop. The key is to show that the product is appropriate to the site combined with appropriateness to the model, who, of course, looks like someone with whom the customer can identify.

René Gnam, President,
René Gnam Consultation Corporation

□

22. Details: If You Can't See Them, You May Not Order the Merchandise

Because the mail-order shopper cannot touch, feel, or examine the merchandise, the photograph must supply as much clarification in these areas as possible. If the customer cannot see your merchandise, you're expecting a great deal to hope that a purchase will be made. One of the major responsibilities of the art director and photographer is to question whether or not the artwork (photography) has depicted the texture of the merchandise. Velvet must look like velvet, wood must appear like wood, metal must be metal. One aim of the photograph is to create in the mind of the customer the feel of the merchandise. And often this "feel" is developed by how well the photograph pictures the details of the item. A major fringe benefit, of course, is that the customer also can see what the item looks like.

The photograph from The Very Thing! catalog (Figure 16) forces the customer to struggle in order to see the details of the dress. Even though an attempt is made to indicate the fabric is lace, too many questions are left in the mind of the viewer. Is the bodice lace as well? What does the design really look like? Where are the details of the structure and pattern? The copy description answers many of these points, but the photograph does not "entice" with enough *details* to make the customer want to read the description. In addition, not only is the merchandise hard to see, but the copy is hard to read because it's overprinted on a photographic background that varies from dark to light.

Some excellent planning went into the coordination between layout and copy, so it's particularly unfortunate that the presentation has not worked hard enough to motivate the customer. For example, the last copy line is "Black purse and bow pin sold on page

Figure 16

Figure 17

portion of it occupies the frame, and one cannot discern its material. The copy tells us it is black ribbed silk, but its details cannot be seen. How could the dress or purse have been photographed more effectively? A studio session rather than an outdoor location would have allowed more lighting control for the garment. This dress needed plenty of light thrown on the front of it (probably from an angle) to delineate that it is full of tiny tucks and interspersed with bands of lace (copy tells us this). The purse also could have used angled lighting in order to cast enough shadow/highlight contrast to bring out the ribbing. Because black items are difficult to photograph, they require more forethought than usual. But no matter what the color of your merchandise or the material of which it's made, it must be seen to be appreciated. Remember, the only "grabber" you've got for that product is its picture.

Cecile Wood Gort, President, Gortwood Associates

8." This normally would be an excellent cross-reference to boost sales. But one has to peer at the photograph to discover that the model seems to be holding these items in her right hand.

In the photograph from page eight of this catalog (Figure 17) the purse is difficult to see, since only a

23. Your Choice of Type Can Enhance or Confuse Your Catalog

One vehicle through which your message gets to your consumer is the typeface of your catalog. Graphics may attract and copy may sell, but it's the legibility of the type that moves your customer from paragraph to paragraph to make the sale. You should ask yourself three questions when you review layouts for an upcoming promotion:

1. How will the type reproduce against the background design?

2. What color will the type be printed in? Will that color be easy to read?

3. Is the type legible?

Backgrounds

In their quest for creativity, designers sometimes prepare layouts using bold colors and designs against which type can be lost. Because catalogs offer limited space, most type is set small—in 6 or 8 point size. Deep background colors like navy blue, burgundy, or dark grey can create havoc when type is reproduced against them.

When designers submit a layout for approval, they indicate type areas with thin horizontal lines (see Figure 18) drawn in black, indicating that type will print over the background color, or white, indicating that type will be dropped out of the background. But when type is set, these thin lines are replaced by blocks of type that can create a completely different—sometimes unattractive—appearance.

Blocks of type placed against dark backgrounds must be "dropped out"—another technique that can cause problems. If your typeface is too small or too thin, it will "fill in" when printed and reproduce out of

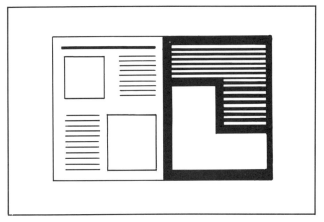

Figure 18

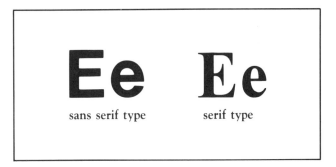

sans serif type   serif type

Figure 19

register. Because color plates are out of exact alignment, the type will contain hues of different colors and be very difficult to read. Horizontal or diagonal background patterns can cause even worse problems.

Type Color

Designers sometimes specify that type be printed in a light color like grey, yellow, or mustard. Small type will have less impact in these colors, and can reproduce very badly. It's wise to use a strong, sans serif Gothic face (Figure 19) in these situations. Gothic typefaces have an overall even weight with little contrast between thick and thin strokes. Helvetica, Futura and News Gothic are all good choices. If serif faces are used, designers should choose a bold type and consider appropriate leading and letterspacing to enhance readability.

ascender **k g** descender

Figure 20

Legibility

Legibility is greatly affected by leading and lettering spaces. To establish a mood, a designer may choose a serif typeface with large ascenders or descenders (Figure 20). If the face is delicate and the type must reproduce in small sizes, the serifs can fill in or break off, giving the type an unfinished appearance. In some typefaces, the ascenders and descenders can touch. Additional leading can "clean up" the look. Adding space between words or letters can also improve the type's appearance and readability.

□

24. Ten Ways to Improve Your Order Form

A well-designed order form can encourage order placement, while a poorly designed form actually has the opposite effect. Here are 10 tips to help you maximize your order form's function.

1. Keep it clean. Use lots of white space. Keep your form open and attractive. An order form that looks complicated *is* complicated. This can result in missing or wrong information . . . or keep your customer from placing the order at all.

2. Leave room to write. Make your form easy to fill out. If necessary, increase the form's size to assure the order's legibility.

3. Remember your order entry system. The form should be compatible with your order entry system, especially if your system is computerized. A form with the same design as your computer format will speed order entry and fulfillment, while reducing input errors.

4. Put the order form where it can be found. Try to place it in the catalog's center or as an outer wrap. An order form split between signatures is confusing and difficult to find.

5. Keep it simple. Color can be confusing and distracting. Use basic black or some other dark color for important information. Colors should be used to highlight and enhance.

6. Attract attention. Use screens of black or second colors where you want to draw attention or create sections, but watch complementary colors. Shade the areas you don't want filled in. Use screens sparingly.

7. Find out where to ship the order. Always ask for "ship to" information or a gift address. If you can offer a gift card, it's an added touch your customer will appreciate.

8. Ask customers to use the label. Remind people to affix mailing labels in the proper place on the order form—important for tracking codes. Try to reduce your costs by asking recipients of multiple catalogs to return the labels so you can eliminate duplicates from your lists.

9. Explain your exchange policy. Provide specifics on returns and exchanges, including postage. The FTC is becoming increasingly strict about this requirement.

10. Reinforce your guarantee. The order form is an ideal place to restate your guarantee. It can instill confidence in a customer about to place an order.

Joyce Kole, Catalog Accounts Manager, Webcraft, Inc.

25. Keeping Your Identity When Publishing a Sale Catalog

Naturally the decision to have a sale has been discussed at length and the reasons for having it have been determined. Often these reasons can guide the creative staff in developing that sale look.

It's not unusual to see a company mix sale items and regularly priced merchandise in its standard publication. The sale items will have attention called to them with boldface type saying "SALE," or with the regular price crossed out and a handwritten, lower price scripted in next to it in a contrasting color. Depending on the catalog's image, these techniques can be handled subtly and with some elegance or in a bolder, louder manner. In either case, it is not difficult for the catalog to retain its usual identity, because the sale items are embraced within the pages of the regular publication. The effect created upon the customer is secondary, not unlike shopping in a retail store where a few racks are "marked down."

But what happens when an entire book is devoted to a sale? When the whole store is a bargain basement? The catalog marketer should carefully consider three questions.

1. Should we change our look to say "sale"? (After all, the entire book could be printed with crossed-out prices.) *How* can we say it?

2. How can we *differentiate* a sale book from our usual style and image? And *how far* should we go?

3. Should we change that style and image? And in the case of a catalog which generally uses a creative style that is subtle: can we? Should we merge our usual style with the louder overtones implied by an entire sale book?

Naturally, one of the first questions you should ask yourself is "Will a sale eat into our usual profits? Will our customers wait for the sale, come to expect

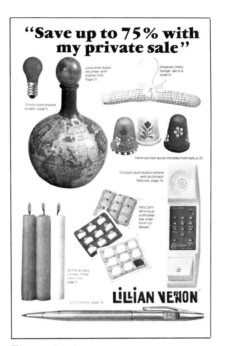

Figure 21-A

it, only purchase from us during it?" One viewpoint is positive. Retail stores use sales effectively and profitably, so why shouldn't catalogers? The other viewpoint expresses the danger of wooing a different kind of customer with a sale book than with the regular book. What happens if the cataloger's customer profile begins to bend and twist with names that only want bargains, or that respond to a different look and feeling? This is the main reason to maintain the same style in your sale catalog and your regular book. Any new names will respond to the same style and probably convert quite well into "regular" customers. (The exception to this attitude would be if the cataloger consciously wished to develop a new segment. But there would be other, better ways of going about that.)

Figure 21 (A–D) shows an all-sale catalog published by the Lillian Vernon Corporation. The creation of this book is a marvel, because it preserves the Vernon look and style, yet accomplishes this with a different layout, an adjustment of the grid, and other subtleties. It says "sale" everywhere, but says it distinctly (and distinctively) a la Vernon.

Figure 21-B

Figure 21-C

Figure 21-D

Let's begin with the cover (see Figure 21-A). It digresses from its usual style (see Figure 21-B), but is careful to choose a headline type style (the serifs help) that is dominant, but doesn't scream "cheap." The wording is thoughful, too: combining an impressive 75 percent with "*my* private sale," engenders a feeling of warmth, personality, and exclusivity (again, the Vernon image). The Vernon logo is prominent and the cover layout echoes the page layout of the usual catalog with which the customers are familiar.

Comparing the interior pages of the sale catalog (Figure 21-C) and the regular catalog (Figure 21-D) shows how carefully the same image has been adhered to in the sale book. Adding grid lines makes the sale book different and less casual, but preserves the asymmetrical look of the regular catalog. Notice that, even though these items are on sale, they are not crammed onto the pages. Keeping the same number of items per page as the regular catalog maintains the Vernon feeling.

There is no doubt that Vernon customers will respond to this book with enthusiasm, and any new hands into which it falls will convert quite nicely to a regular Vernon customer. Plenty of thanks can go to the thoughtful creative development, which took a marketing idea and merchandised it within firm disciplines to express with its graphics the appropriate style desired.

□

26. Minor Alterations to Regular Art and Copy: An Inexpensive Way to Present Sale Merchandise

Utilizing the art and copy used in your regular catalog for a sales vehicle will save you money. Nothing (or very little) need be spent in the creative or production area on new photographs or line drawings. Generally, the same color separations can be used, eliminating a catalog preparation cost. Changes in copy are often negligible as well. These cost reductions become significant in a sale catalog, especially

Figure 22

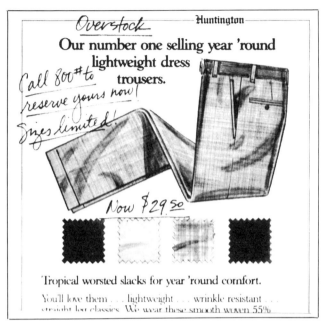

Figure 23

when the lower sale price reduces your individual product profit margin.

Figure 22 from the Williams-Sonoma Catalog for Cooks shows how a photograph used for a regular catalog listing of one-quarter of a page has been cropped identically, but reduced to fit a listing of one-sixth of a page. The copy is the same, too; only the first and last sentence in the body copy of the sale version have been eliminated. Using the sale banner across the top of the ad is a very effective attention-getting device.

Another example, this one from the Huntington Clothiers Summer sale catalog (Figure 23) shows how the original art can be cleverly overlaid with a hand-written sales announcement. The handwriting is reproduced in an ink-colored blue that gives the impression of being freshly marked on the page. The effectiveness of this technique is obvious at a glance. The "bargain" impact is strengthened by letting the customer see a "real" ad at the original price, while attention is captured by altering the original version with handwriting.

Both techniques are valuable because they combine effective presentations with cost savings.

Lou Smith, President,
Lou E. Smith Associates

☐

27. Interim Mailings: Is There a Creative Approach That's Right for You?

The possibilities for testing the feasibility of interim mailings are endless. Consider just a few alternatives:

● Filled with your best items, brochures or mini-catalogs can be mailed to your best customers in between your full-scale catalog mailings.

Community Café
"The Coffee Connoisseurs'Exchange"

Aug. 1983

The Saga of the Coffee Bean In America

There have been many fascinating tales—both mythical and true—relating to the origins of coffee and its spread throughout the world. One of the most extraordinary, and widely accepted, is the saga of a royal tree that literally sowed its beans around the world.

During the late 17th and early 18th centuries, coffee was an exotic beverage sought out by the rich and fashionable nobility of Europe. At that time coffee trees grew only in Africa, India and the Dutch West Indian colony of Java where they were highly prized and the seeds were jealously guarded. A tropical plant that didn't thrive in Europe, it held an insatiable curiosity for King Louis XIV of France who adored luxuries and had become a profound coffee drinker. Through various diplomatic means, he convinced the Dutch to give him a coffee tree for the royal gardens. The tree arrived in Paris around 1715, and a special greenhouse (the first in Europe) was built for it in the Jardin des Plantes. It was this sturdy five-footer that held the seeds of Latin America's coffee future.

A French officer stationed in Martinique, Gabriel Mathieu de Clieu, saw the tree and envisioned its cultivation in the colonies. Unable to obtain seedlings from the royal botanist, he stole them one night and set sail for the New World. Thus, the history of coffee was about to undergo its greatest change.

The journey to the New World posed many dangers, especially to the young tree. But De Clieu, enthralled with his dream of coffee in Martinique, managed to get it home and nourished it in his garden where it did exceedingly well. From one noble tree, coffee crops spread throughout Martinique and the adjacent islands. It was a prized crop and each colony jealously guarded the seedlings. Export was forbidden under pain of death.

In 1727, a boundary dispute arose between Dutch and French Guiana, both coffee-producing colonies. Francisco de Melo Palheta, a lieutenant in the Brazilian army, was sent to help mediate a treaty. His mission was successful in more ways than one...both political and social. Through a rather seductive series of proceedings, he was able to convince the grateful wife of the French Guiana's Governor

to slip him some coffee seedlings in a farewell bouquet. As a result of this great diplomatic coup, Brazil became the greatest coffee producing country.

Descendants of the French tree spread from Brazil to Hawaii in 1825 and were brought back to Africa by Roman Catholic missionaries in the 1890's, completing an odyssey that had taken it around the world.

Coffee of the Month: Bourbon Santos, Araraquarense Zone

"There's an awful lot of coffee in Brazil" go the words of a once popular song. And so it is, as this is the nation that made coffee famous. Most of the blends we drink in America contain at least some Brazilian coffee, which is noted for its distinctive aroma and full body.

Some Brazilians are superior (our Sao Paulo District is an excellent example) and others, with limited availability, may rate even higher for their unique flavor. The Bourbon Santos, Araraquarense we are offering this month contains the essence of the finest Brazil has to offer, an experience that should appeal to the novice as well as the connoisseur.

Grown in the Araraquarense zone situated in the mid-west of the state of Sao Paulo near the port of Santos, the Bourbon Arabica tree is cultivated at an altitude of 2800 feet in very fertile soil. As with most Brazilian coffees, it is processed by the sun drying method. It's the world's oldest method of preparing the beans for roasting, requiring careful and time-consuming controls.

The coffee we are offering this month is selected, bold beans—premium graded ones that are generally reserved for the European market and rarely become available here. Our Community Bourbon Santos, Araraquarense is then roasted to a medium darkness that unfolds its unique Brazilian flavor. Rich and robust with a special smoothness and clarity, it has no bitter after-taste. Ideal as an after-dinner coffee, you might compare it to a full-flavored red wine. Please order 3 lbs. for $13.50.

Traveling Refreshed

One of the handiest thermal carafes we've come across is this one by Nissan. It has a unique stainless steel liner that's unbreakable and thermally efficient. The shell is molded of a very durable plastic with stainless steel trim and is so sturdy that the whole carafe is warrantied for five

Figure 24

- They can be a way of attracting new customers without the cost of a large catalog.

- They can be developed to test new items before you add them to your main book.

- An entire series can be produced to target various segments of your list, one for kitchen items, another for pet products, a third for stationery, and so on.

- They can be used to test new creative concepts or new merchandising concepts, without distrubing the familiarity of your large catalog.

Some Favorite Thoughts For Your Holiday Dinners

There's a special joy to dining in South Louisiana where family cooking traditions are an art of the ages. Each year, as the holiday season approaches, we sift through our files of recipes collected throughout the years. One we've enjoyed many times is for an orange-ginger sauce that we serve with Christmas roast duck. Prepared with our Community Kitchens Orange Marmalade, it truly lends a festive touch to dinner and we think you'll enjoy it too. We like to serve the duck with fresh cooked broccoli that's blanketed with a cheese horseradish sauce (spiced with our Community Kitchens Horseradish Mustard). For dessert, our Community Whiskey Cake is a hands-down winner. Serve it with fresh whipped cream garnished with shaved chocolate...and a piping hot cup of our famous coffee. The 8" Irish Whiskey Cake is 2½ lbs. and costs $22.50. On our table, a presentation is as important as the taste of food. That's why we were especially pleased to find this set of full-lead crystal dessert plates imported from France by J.G. Durand. As beautiful as they are, they're also quite durable and dishwasher safe. The set of one 12½" platter plus six 7½" individual plates is $44.00.

ORANGE-GINGER SAUCE FOR CHRISTMAS DUCK

2 ducks, roasted according to instructions provided on the wrapper or use your favorite method.
¾ cup Community Kitchens Orange Marmalade
¼ to ½ cup orange juice
1 teaspoon finely minced fresh ginger
1 teaspoon lemon juice
1 tablespoon sherry

Just before serving the ducks, place orange marmalade, lemon and orange juices and ginger in a saucepan. Heat and slowly stir until the mixture is smooth and well blended. Add sherry. If sauce is too thick, add a small amount of orange juice until desired thickness is obtained.

Figure 25

- They can be used as seasonal supplements to your product line.

- As a way of developing customer anticipation, they can include special values, discount coupons, and other incentives to ordering.

- Customer loyalty and a "family" feeling (and consequently, sales) can be enhanced through uniquely designed mailings to promote highly specialized product lines, such as a newsletter promotion to collectors, gourmet cheese buyers, or coffee lovers.

One of the really interesting approaches to the final item on this list is in Figure 24. This piece has the flavor of a newsletter rather than a promotional mailing. It is printed on newsletter-style paper in a single color, brown. It folds into three panels plus an attached ordering envelope and is a self-mailer, so the physical style is neat and convenient. This mailing is a supplement to the main catalogs from Community Kitchens and Community Coffee. Though the format

GOURMET FOODS

COMMUNITY PRESERVES
- ☐ **13a.** Oregon Red Raspberry – 26 oz. $12.50 #8-4158
- ☐ **13b.** With Crate $14.00 #8-4204
- ☐ **13c.** Fancy Sunripened Strawberry – 26 oz. $12.50 #8-4131
- ☐ **13d.** With Crate $14.00 #8-4212
- ☐ **13e.** Oregon Black Raspberry – 26 oz. $12.50 #8-4166
- ☐ **13f.** With Crate $14.00 #8-4220
- ☐ **13g.** Fancy Oregon Blackberry – 26 oz. $12.50 #8-4107
- ☐ **13h.** With Crate $14.00 #8-4190
- ☐ **13k.** Michigan Red-Tart Cherry – 26 oz. $12.50 #8-4123
- ☐ **13m.** With Crate $14.00 #8-4174
- ☐ **13n.** Bittersweet Orange Marmalade – 26 oz. $12.50 #8-4115
- ☐ **13p.** With Crate $14.00 #8-4182

14a. CHOCOLATE KRUNCH
- ☐ (3) 7½ oz. jars $10.75 #8-6088
- ☐ (6) 7½ oz. jars $19.75 #8-6096
- ☐ (9) 7½ oz. jars $29.50 #8-6118

MUSTARD
- ☐ Choose (3) 7 oz. jars $10.75 #8-2783
  - ☐ **16a.** Toasted Onion #44377
  - ☐ **16b.** Horseradish #44385
  - ☐ **16c.** Jalepeno #44393
  - ☐ **16d.** Sesame #44369
  - ☐ **16e.** Teriyaki #44350

SYRUP
- ☐ **16f.** Cane Syrup 3-12 oz. bottles #8-2791 $10.00 ($3.34 ea.)
- ☐ **16g.** Maple Syrup 2-12 oz. bottles #8-2805 $12.50 ($6.25 ea.)
- ☐ **16h.** Syrup Assortment 1 Maple & 2 Cane 3-12 oz. bottles #8-2813 $12.50

VINEGAR & OIL
- ☐ **17a.** Chardonnay 1-26.5 oz. bottle #8-4387 $11.50
- ☐ **17b.** Chardonnay 3-26.5 oz. bottles #8-4395 $26.75 ($8.92 ea.)
- ☐ **17c.** Cabernet Sauvignon 1-26.5 oz. bottle #8-4360 $11.50
- ☐ **17d.** Cabernet Sauvignon 3-26.5 oz. bottles #8-4379 $26.75 ($8.92 ea.)
- ☐ **17e.** Extra Virgin Olive Oil 1-26.5 oz. bottle #8-4409 $14.50
- ☐ **17f.** Extra Virgin Olive Oil 3-26.5 oz. bottles #8-4417 $35.75 ($11.92 ea.)

- ☐ **17g.** Vinegar and Oil Assortment. Includes one bottle each of 17a, 17c, 17e $29.50 #8-4425

WHISKEY CAKE
- ☐ **17h.** 2½ Pound Cake $22.50 #8-4301

BELGIAN CHOCOLATES
- ☐ **17s-a.** One-1 lb. box $19.75 #8-6266

FUDGE CRUNCH
- ☐ **17s-b.** One-1 lb. box $13.75 #8-4263
- ☐ **17s-c.** Two-1 lb. boxes $25.75 #8-4298
- ☐ **17s-d.** Three-1 lb. boxes $37.75 #8-4271

CAFE CREMES
- ☐ **17s-e.** One-13oz. box $12.50 #8-3801
- ☐ **17s-f.** Two-13 oz. boxes $23.75 #8-3860
- ☐ **17s-g.** Three-13 oz. boxes $34.75 #8-3798

TOTALLY NUTS
- ☐ **17s-h.** 1½ pound can $17.95 #8-6134

MOSTLY NUTS
- ☐ **17s-k.** 2 pound can $14.50 #8-6142

CHOCOLATE LACE
- ☐ **17s-m.** 20 oz. can $11.75 #8-6274

TOTAL $ _____

HOLIDAY GIFTS

TREASURE CHESTS
- ☐ **17s-n.** Three-7½ oz. jars of Chocolate Krunch $19.50 #8-6401
- ☐ **17s-p.** One-1 lb. box of Fudge Crunch and one 7½ oz. jar of Chocolate Krunch $26.75 #8-6428
- ☐ **17s-r.** Three-7 oz. jars of Gourmet Mustard $20.50 #8-6436
- ☐ **17s-s.** Three-13.25 oz. bottle assortment of Wine Vinegar and Extra Virgin Olive Oil. $22.75 #8-6282

BOUNTIFUL BASKETS
- ☐ **17s-t.** Louisiana Gourmet Basket $26.75 #8-6231
- ☐ **17s-u.** Gourmet Syrup Basket $22.50 #8-6258
- ☐ **17s-v.** The Breakfast Hamper $36.75 #8-6223

TOTAL $ _____

Figure 26

of the mailing is unique, its mood does not differ greatly from that created by the catalogs. These begin with about ten pages telling about "South Louisiana's Community Kitchens" and the unforgettable dining moments which occur in that part of the country. A history is given of the family that developed Community coffee. Various styles of roasting, grinding and brewing are described. It has much of the feel of a tour-guide publication, the kind you would find at the sales desk after touring a famous historical building.

So the talky, friendly approach of the newsletter is not far afield from the catalog, even though the format is entirely different. The "articles" found in this newsletter are oriented toward sales, but the items sold are preambled with "newsy" copy and recipes (see Figure 25). Though this approach is unusual, it should work extremely well with this product line, which is so distinctly oriented toward coffees and gourmet dining. People who are interested in these areas are almost like club members, so the newsletter becomes a strong supplement to their interests.

The newsletter suffers from one liability. It is difficult to match the items spoken about in the "arti-

cles" to their positions on the order form. Figure 26 shows the section of the order form that matches the items spoken about in Figure 25. But it is difficult to locate the items in the article—no graphic element was used to highlight the featured item. There is no key number or other reference to help the customer locate the item on the order form. Usually a form which preprints the items and prices does so for the customer's convenience and the company's own order-entry ease. But in this case, for every customer who ordered an item, one has to wonder how many got tired of looking for it and dropped the promotion in the wastebasket. And suppose the customer wanted two whiskey cakes and three bottles of olive oil. There is no place on the form to easily indicate "how many" and no place to easily add up an order.

This excellent promotional idea fell apart in the important final step—the ordering vehicle. Because it is so confusing, sales have surely been lost. The back of the order form, by the way, lists an assortment of ground coffees, coffee beans and tea from the regular line. This excellent idea should encourage the steady customer to place an order for an old favorite or try a new flavor in addition to purchasing one of the new items in the newsletter.

With any promotion, keep this in mind: if you offer the right products to the right people at the right prices, you will probably make the sale—unless you place roadblocks in the way, like making it difficult to order. Although only Community Coffee knows whether this newsletter paid its way, it can almost unequivocably be said that it would have been more effective if the order form had been clearer.

☐

CHAPTER THREE

Developing, Choosing, and Testing Effective Lists

WITHOUT A GOOD MAILING LIST, YOUR CATALOG WILL never reach all the customers who wish to buy your merchandise.

The art of choosing a list, and the scientific methods used to refine the list business, are outlined in the next chapter.

☐

28. Establishing a Mailing List

You've investigated direct marketing, have seen that it is growing more rapidly than other retail sales methods and have decided that you want some of the action. You've chosen the product or service you wish to offer and now the problem is . . . to whom do you present your offer? How do you acquire names that are likely to become your customers?

There is no one correct way to develop a mailing list, of course. Many methods and types of lists are available. But one source, however, must be considered: your own "house" list.

Your present customers qualify for a house mailing list. If you ever have offered the same, or similar, items or services through retail approaches, then you have a nucleus of customers who have proven a need or desire for your offer; could use additional or supplemental goods or services; have an appreciation of your reliability and the quality of your offerings. These customers become your prospective house mailing list.

How do you get their names and addresses? At a retail establishment, when payment is made (by credit card, cash or check), ask for an address. If the customer requires an explanation, honestly explain that you would like to add his or her name to your mailing list so you can keep customers abreast of your latest offers. If you advertise in newspapers or magazines offering a discount coupon requiring redemption at the store, you can design the coupon so that customers must complete it with their names and addresses.

But beware: lists of retail store buyers may not be the strongest prospects for mail-order sales, because these names are not proven respondents to mail-order promotions. Advertising in newspapers or magazines with a coupon that can be used to make purchases by mail is a better way to develop reliable lists.

The object is to build your house file. When you rent names from outside sources, your short term objective is to find lists that will increase your sales at the time of rental. Anyone who purchases something from you through a rented list becomes your name, so the long term objective is to increase and improve your house file.

☐

29. To Whom Should You Mail? And How Many of Those Names Should Be Rented?

These questions are of vital and constant interest to catalog marketers. Obviously the answers are extremely varied, depending on many factors, some of which will be unique to your specific business. A few of the qualifications that will affect your decisions are

- the size of your house customer file,
- the profitability of mailings to the house file,
- the percentage of attrition of the house file each year (customers who stop responding), and
- your specific interest in wanting to achieve a house file of a particular size.

Let's assume a house active file of 1,000,000 customer names that includes customers who have ordered from you at least once in the last thirty months. (Some mailers consider "house active file" to include only twenty-four-month names; some use thirty-six months.) Then assume six mailings per year for a total of 6,000,000 pieces, with a net-net profit of $100 per thousand pieces mailed. This provides a profit of $600,000 and is based on a conservative overall response rate of $1000 per thousand. Many mailers have response rates far in excess of this.

Now let's assume a house active file yearly attrition rate of 18 percent. One hundred and eighty thousand names will be lost; so just to stay "even," 180,000 new names must be developed. Assuming *all* new customers are achieved *only* through rented list mailings, and these lists will have a response rate of 3 percent, then 6,000,000 rented list names would have to be used. If you had a loss on these names of $50 per thousand names mailed, a loss of $300,000 would be involved. Pit this against your profit of $600,000 on your house list mailing, and you net an overall profit of $300,000.

The true measurement of potential and actual response rate income varies greatly, with a large portion depending on the average order size. Some companies operate profitably with a $15 to $20 average order. Many in the giftware field are in the $40 to $60 average order size.

Much effort is being put forth by catalog marketers to improve response rates from rented lists, generally by a much more intricate selection process.

This includes more detailed segmentation programs to identify those parts of lists available that will provide the desired response rates in both percentage of response and average order size.

Because names achieved through rented list mailings can be very expensive, most mailers rely heavily upon media advertising, as well as "send us the names of your friends" approaches and inserts in packages of other mailers. Detailed "cost-per-name" records must be kept for every approach used. Most important is to keep detailed data on the following:

1. What is a new name really worth to you? What is the average income for one year, two years, three years, etc., of every new name added to the file?

2. What are the differences in cost and average income of names recruited via each new name recruitment program?

In the final analysis, don't be guided by what someone says is the ideal proportion of mailings to rented lists versus mailing to house file names. Instead, consider all recruitment approaches used and then decide the number of new names needed to replace those lost through attrition, plus the number desired to increase house file size, all at costs that provide a satisfactory bottom line profit.

R. Roy Hedberg, President, Hedberg & Associates

30. Where Do You Go to Find Good Lists?

Finding good lists is a perpetual problem for any catalog program. No sooner has one catalog dropped than it's time for the next one. Often the lists for the second mailing must be chosen before the results are in from the first one. And sometimes one test list seems to work well enough to be rolled out, but for some reason the roll-out is unprofitable.

Most catalogers use response lists (lists composed of actual mail-order buyers or inquirers) rather than compiled lists (names assembled by scanning telephone books or other directories). Historically, response lists have produced a higher percentage of response, enough to justify a cost almost double that of compiled lists.

Typically, the main proponents of compiled lists have been employees or agents of the companies which compile the lists. Response lists are preferred by brokers, who earn higher commissions on lists costing $65 per thousand names than lists costing $35 per thousand. But whether the lists are compiled or response, the cataloger wants files that work.

Over the years, the balance has tipped in favor of response lists. Response lists already have weeded out those people who will *never* buy through direct mail. This eliminates perhaps 20 percent of the people who would be unprofitable to any mailer, but who show up time and again in compiled lists. Also, because response lists are made up of buyers who can be selected by recency of purchase, it's possible to rent response lists where every address has been verified within the past few months.

But response lists are not trouble-free. List renters do not always anticipate the mercurial marketing plans of some list owners. If a marketer of $100 widgets has put together a responsive list which you've tested and found profitable, you might decide to roll out to the entire 100,000-name file. Imagine your surprise when you find that the marketer has begun selling $1.50 gizmos, and that 75 percent of the file is now made up of those low-priced buyers.

The ideal, of course, would be to pay the rates charged for compiled lists, yet obtain names which are as resposive as response lists. It's possible now, through regression analysis techniques, to eliminate unprofitable segments of compiled lists, and to perform roll-outs on profitable segments without paying the high prices of response lists.

What's regression analysis? It's mathematical wizardry. You may remember from your college statistics class that regression analysis is "a technique by which the conditional expectation of one of two correlated variables is closer to the mean of its set than are given values of the second to the mean of its set." Got it? Happily, you don't have to, because statisticians can do the work for you. You merely need to know that it is a comparison of the importance of a number of variables (the characteristics of a compiled list) to the overall profitability of your mailing. You will select for your roll-out only those segments of the list which the analysis tells you are contributing to its success.

This service actually costs far less than you might think. If you're mailing more than a couple hundred thousand catalogs a year, your overall list cost will be far less than the cost of mailing to response lists.

Marshall Hamilton, Marketing Director, Phillips Publications

31. What You'll Want to Know When Ordering a List

When you order a mailing list, there are three ways you can classify information: must-know data, need-to-know data, and nice-to-know data.

Here's what the "must-know" category covers:

- kind and classification of names
- format required
- selection factors available
- how names will be used
- when names will be needed

Price is not in the "must-know" category. It may not even be a "need-to-know" item if the list is going to be utilized in any case.

With must-know data in hand, consider the following for best results:

1. Be certain you are on the same wavelength as your list supplier. If you order insurance names, do you wish to select executives by name and title at large companies? Home offices, branch offices, general agents, consultants, pension plan specialists, or adjusters? Broker offices and agencies or brokers and agents? One per establishment? Life or Casualty? Geographic segmentation?

2. Treat your list supplier as one of your privileged professional consultants, and tell all. The more your list supplier knows about what you have done and are doing, the better her suggestions can be. This means confiding not only which lists worked and which didn't, but the precise response to each. If your list supplier isn't worth treating as your consultant, find one that is. This can pay off handsomely.

3. If a list will be used several more times per year, see if you can buy the names outright. Or, at the very least, attempt to work out a discount for the additional uses.

4. Use 5th digit and 4th and 5th digit of ZIP to select test samples. Every test is (or should be) made with the hope that it will be successful and that it will lead to a roll-out. The best way to prevent duplication on a roll-out is to select by fifth digit of ZIP. This is safe, sure, economical and simple. It's easy to record such usage, and it's easy for the list owner to comply with such selection and omission.

Most Nth number select programs have no way of guaranteeing this, unless the computer service has a sophisticated program that tags each record used. The computer cannot identify records taken, and thus cannot skip them. If a list is updated between uses in any way, even by the removal or addition of just one record, there is no way to guarantee that the test sample won't be mailed again.

Last digit ZIP also lets you retest or reuse the records tested the first time. Whereas one for 10, one

for 15 or one for 20 selection will not provide sufficient sampling through the entire list, use of the last two digits of ZIP will.

Abiding by these suggestions will improve your chances of success, but keep in mind that no matter where you start, you come back to the nexus—the need for testing.

Ed Burnett, President, Ed Burnett Consultants, Inc.

☐

32. Why Should You Test Mailing Lists?

Testing is the only commonsense way to locate the best prospects among a plethora of lists. Because nothing stands still, there's no end to testing. People change, tastes and lifestyles change, competitors change—and offers, campaigns and marketing concepts must meet these challenges.

The overall rule is to test, retest and then retest your retests. Never stop testing, because every mailing, every insertion, every phone campaign can and should be part of a learning curve. Testing must be a continuous process, not something added to the mix now and again. If it's not a regular part of your program, you'll lose more than its cost through misdirected promotions. Testing should be designed with two goals in mind:

- Determine which activities will produce more profit—and do more

- Determine which activities will produce less profit—and do fewer (or perhaps none)

Most direct-mail testing relates to prospecting. There are four ways to improve the bottom line:

1. Increase the response per M mailed

Total costs of Item A, excluding promotional costs	$8/unit	An increase of 2 orders/M mailed, (2/10 of 1%)	adds $57/M
Selling price	$30/unit	An increase from 1.3 units per order to 1.4 units per order	adds $22/M
Order margin	$22/unit	A decrease in unit cost from $8 to	
Cost in the mail	$220/M	$7 per unit	adds $13/M
Average response (10 orders/M)	1.0%	A decrease in cost to mail	adds $10/M
Average order size	1.3 units per order		

2. Increase the average size of the order

3. Increase the order margin (gross profit) per order by increasing price and decreasing cost of goods sold

4. Decrease the costs by decreasing the cost of promotion and by decreasing costs of handling order fulfillment

A careful examination of these methods leads to two simple rules:

1. Never stop trying to increase the total dollars from a given effort through obtaining greater response, higher average order size, or increased order margin.

2. Never stop trying to reduce the costs of doing business, as long as the customer is served well and honestly.

At some point, once costs have been shaved and the order margin fairly well set, the leverage in direct mail essentially comes down to ways and means of increasing the response rate. A small increase in response can translate into a remarkably high increase in profit and return on your investment. The difference between success and failure can be as fine as one- or two-tenths of a percentage point. Let's look at a fairly typical example.

Here, an increase of just two orders per M (from 1.3M to 1.5M) is greater than the combined additions from the other indicated changes. And it's usually easier to find ways to increase the number of orders, at any point, than to get comparable bottom-line improvement through factors affecting gross profit on a

per-order basis. Remember, we have examined just the raw cost of adding a customer to the rolls, not the variable worth of different types of new customers.

Ed Burnett, President, Ed Burnett Consultants, Inc.

□

33. Testing: The Heart of Mail Order

You can't be involved with catalogs or direct mail promotions for very long with very much success if you haven't discovered the art of testing. Every catalog marketer worthy of the name is involved in a continuous process of improving the average response rate with the least expenditure and the least risk. This is not to say that brilliant strokes are not conceived and accomplished from time to time, but the sane marketer builds into his programs a percentage of allowance for these "risky" moves, and that percentage is small.

There are a number of rules for proper testing:

1. Do not be guilty of the "continuous series of one experiment" syndrome. This is the old story of "do you have ten years of experience—or one year of experience ten times?" In a "continuous series of one experiment," one offer in one package is sent to one list—and "results" are recorded. At the very least,

four or five separate list concepts or segments should be tested.

2. Once established, a "control" package (your standard offer) should never be retired—until you have created a new "control" that outpulls the old.

3. Confirm any successful list test with a "continuation" consisting of some modest multiple of the test. If a test of 5,000 from a list of several hundred thousand looks promising, test five more cross-section lots of 5,000—not one lot of 25,000. What you are looking for here is confirmation of results. The smaller the variance from the mean (the average of all 25,000, in this case) the greater your confidence can be that a large continuation—say 50,000 or 100,000—will work as well.

Ed Burnett, President, Ed Burnett Consultants, Inc.

☐

34. Regression Analysis Techniques: A Way to Make Compiled Lists More Responsive

The technique of regression analysis is not new: it's a standard statistical tool for comparing the relative behavior of two or more variables. But now this technique is being applied to the behavior of list segments in a way that promises to make compiled lists work as well as response lists, but at a much lower cost.

When you use a compiled list, it has been developed by people who, for example, pore over telephone yellow pages and other directories to find the names and addresses of every person in a specific category. In years past, the name and address were about all the compilers really knew.

Today, compilers capture much more information. Just by knowing the ZIP code for every name on

the list, compilers have a great deal of data about the segments that work best. An immense body of information exists about the characteristics of individual ZIP codes. For example, through ZIP codes you can tell whether your offer works best in urban, suburban, or rural areas; or which population segments (e.g., towns of 10,000 to 25,000 people) are most profitable.

To benefit from regression analysis, you must first mail to a defined segment of the universe of names available. Using your past experience in marketing your product, you select broad groupings of possible prospects, perhaps 2,000,000 to 5,000,000 names. You then mail an offer to a portion of your defined universe which is large enough to generate a response of at least 300 orders. If you expect a response of 2 percent, you must mail at least 15,000 names. Most mailers receive a much lower response rate to a prospect offer. Because the test will be invalid if 300 responses are not received, this is no time to be stingy. In fact, you might mail a quantity of about 100,000 names, so a response rate as low as 0.5 percent will give you 500 responses.

Identifying those responses is the key to analysis. Each response is linked back to the data base from which your test names came. After tabulating the data, clusters of response are identified. Through the regression analysis formula, different list characteristics are given scores, indicating the propensity of other list segments with similar characteristics to respond to a similar offer. Finally, it is possible to break down the list universe into segments of varying size, with the expected pull for each segment. You might decide to mail the top two segments of the list universe, which might be 25 percent of the total unverise. But by selecting only those segments likely to buy from you, your overall response rate could be double the rate you'd achieve by mailing to the entire universe. Based on your initial universe, this would give you a data base of from 500,000 to 1,250,000 names to draw from as you plan future mailings.

You can obtain this kind of statistical analysis

from companies like Market Data Retrieval, a large list compiler and trailblazer in deep segmentation of compiled lists. Ask your list compiler about regression analysis. Have it explained in detail relative to your specific program.

Marshall Hamilton, Marketing Director, Philips Publications

□

35. The Whys and Hows of Direct Mail Testing

When preparing to construct a modern building, you would be foolish to begin without analyzing test core samples of the underlying soil. And no marketer should "build" any new campaign (or major product launch) before sampling reception in a few "test" markets. In direct mail, there are two primary reasons for adequate test procedures:

- To save you from disaster by assessing viability for a given offer at a minimum expenditure
- To improve your average response rate and thus maximize your net dollar returns

The factors that affect response are just five—and they are the same whether you wish to acquire a buyer, an inquirer, a donor or a subscriber.

1. Copy—the words you use to create your appeal
2. Package—the "attire" your appeal wears
3. Offer—your appeal
4. Timing—when your appeal arrives
5. List—to whom your appeal is directed

After you have a reasonably adequate mailing, these factors can be improved, through careful testing, as follows:

- Copy—about 20 percent
- Package—from 15 to 30 percent
- Offer—from 50 to 200 percent
- Timing—about 20 percent, except at Christmas
- List—from 300 to 1000 percent

This indicates that testing is most productive when offers and lists are varied. If all other factors must be held for budgetary reasons, then you should spend your money testing various list segments.

Ed Burnett, President, Ed Burnett Consultants, Inc.

□

36. How to Select the Number of Names to Test

Assume you've made 100 tests, of 1,000 pieces each, in a list of 100,000 names . . . giving you 100 keys of 1,000 names each. Further assume that average response to your particular offer is 2 percent. This means that on the complete 100M names mailed, you have a response rate of 20/M, or a total of 2,000 responses.

Did each of the 100 tests come in at 2 percent? No. It's logical to assume that some came in under 2 percent, some came in over, and some right at 2 percent. The distribution, irrespective of the list that's used, the offer that's made, or the package put into the mail, will show that some come in below average and some above. This is called a Standard Distribution Curve. It is likely that one of those 1,000-name test cells came in as low as 0.5 to 0.3 percent, and that one, or maybe a couple, came in as high as 3.0 to 4.0 percent. But most probably came in between 1.5 and 2.5 percent. Statisticians say that approximately two-thirds of the responses will come within the basic shoulders of the Standard Distribution Curve.

Under these circumstances, a test resulting in a response rate of 1.5, 1.7, 2.0, 2.1, 2.3 or 2.5 percent is valid. This explains why a test yielding a 1.8 percent response rate can result in a continuation coming in at 1.6, or maybe 2.0. All of the above spread is within the realm of statistical probability. In other words, your first test of 1.8 percent only said that you are likely to come between 1.4 and 2.2 percent in any continuation. It is important to note that you can get an erratic answer from a small sample of the whole.

GENERAL RULE: The minimum number of responses to evaluate a list test is between thirty and forty. If you have an offer which can be expected to produce 1 percent response, or ten orders per 1,000, you need to test 3M or 4M pieces for an adequate test of that specific offer on that particular list.

How do you know what response will be generated? Really, you don't. You have experience, a feel for the offer, some idea of how given lists have worked in the past. You also have one landmark: the responses you need to break even on your particular mailing. If you are selling a desk calculator by mail at $99.95, where the break-even point is at or near 0.4 percent, obviously the number of responses required, thirty to forty, can only result from a list test of 10M to 12M.

At this point, we can answer the question: How does one select how many names to test from a given list? The answer is enough names to break even, and

enough names to give a sufficient response to provide thirty or forty sales, inquiries, leads or answers.

Ed Burnett, President, Ed Burnett Consultants, Inc.

☐

37. List Segmentation Can Improve Response

By dividing your list into identifiable data elements, such as recency, frequency and monetary value, you can track response of these groups and rank their importance to you.

Here's an example of appropriate segmentation for a mailer with a large house file. Each list segment must be assigned its own mailing key as part of the response vehicle for tracking purposes. Although responses can be matched back to the main file fairly effectively, it is more accurate to assign and print the key as an integral part of the name/address label. Increased segmentation also should be used if you feel that response will be affected by other variables like sex, product purchased, space versus catalog, or business versus consumer.

Continue in this fashion until no longer profitable. Incidentally, segments generally should be larger

Segmentation in Order of Priority

Current 6 months	Multi-buyers	Prior 1–2 years	Multi-buyers
Prior 6–12 months	Multi-buyers	Prior 12–18 months	Buyers over $ Average
Current 6 months	Buyers over $ Average	Prior 12–18 months	Buyers under $ Average
Current 6 months	Buyers under $ Average	Prior 18–24 months	Buyers over $ Average
Prior 6–12 months	Buyers over $ Average	Prior 18–24 months	Buyers under $ Average
Prior 6–12 months	Buyers under $ Average	Prior 2–3 years	Multi-buyers
Current 6 months	Inquirers	Prior 24–30 months	Buyers over $ Average
Prior 6–12 months	Inquirers	Prior 24–30 months	Buyers under $ Average

than 1,000, with 10,000 or so allowing you to feel more comfortable with the accuracy of the results. Statistically, the lower the quantities in your segments, the less confident you can be in interpreting results.

And remember, adequate list maintenance *reports* are not a luxury, but an absolute necessity. Maintaining these reports by computer is helpful in building the segments. List reports should be available by key variables, such as sex, recency of last purchase as opposed to cumulative purchase, multi-buyers, etc. When studied as a group, the mailer can observe trends and really have a handle on customer profile. An added advantage is that your list manager is helped in responding to list orders with accurate quantities and can prepare good data cards. This segmentation also expands the number of mailers who can successfully use your mailing list.

Len Schenker, President, Anchor Computer, Inc.

38. Selecting Business-to-Business Lists

"What's new?" is always important, but what's more relevant is "What's out there?" In the world of the business-to-business catalog industry, there are tiers of mailing lists that merit serious consideration from two angles: (1) the characteristics of your product line, and (2) the coverage necessary to develop new customers input to make up for the normal attrition of old customers.

Though the *core* of mail-order merchandising is list selection of established mail-order buyers, you can't stop there! While strong similarities exist be-

tween business catalog marketing and consumer catalog marketing, there also are many significant differences—making the rules of the game profoundly different. The steps to learning and understanding lists in the business-to-business catalog market cover five key categories.

1. Mail-order buyer lists. Start with those most similar to what you're marketing, and talk list rental or list exchange. Be alert to all the R/F/M (Recency, Frequency, Monetary value) factors, data base netname considerations, and seasonal variables that occur in many product lines. Don't forget the bottom line of experience and testing.

2. Qualified trade magazine subscriber lists. These enable you to focus accurately on your potential market. If you're marketing a costly and/or high-tech product, this focus is critical. You can reach key potential buyers vertically by industry—for instance, the rubber and plastics industry—or horizontally; by job titles such as "purchasing management" or "plant engineering supervisors."

3. Compiled lists. This captures the universe of small business by SIC (Standard Industrial Classification) and keeps up with the entry of new businesses. Don't forget! The business catalog business started with and was built on compiled lists when nothing else was available.

4. General executive-name data base lists. These reach special market segments, achieve indepth geographic coverage, and save on computer costs. They possess a natural, built-in mail responsiveness that automatically gives you a good shot at readership interest.

5. Miscellany. Many other pertinent lists exist: lists that contain quality mail responsiveness and, though not right on target, still reach business people who are always on the lookout for something new or eye-catching. Mainly, these lists include seminar attendees, newsletter subscribers, and buyers of management or training literature.

What's new? Market research—taking your own base line of customers and applying one of the sophisticated "overlay" programs to establish priority factors by industry (SIC), company size and job function characteristics. From this, you can ascertain your share of the market and the size of your untapped prospect market.

What isn't so new is the understanding that, when you do an extensive prospect mailing program, you use your own customer file to suppress all your active names from the net-name output of prospects, and record the percentages of matches (hits) between your own file and each of the prospect files. The higher the percentage of hits with any given list, the more certain that particular list will perform well.

Ira Belth, Chairman, Belth Associates, Inc.

39. How to Maximize List Rental Income

The customer details you carefully assemble and refine allow you to play your house list in intricate ways to increase profits with every mailing. This information also makes your names more valuable to others, and should be monitored continually to keep your list vital and effective. Two other important areas (which often suffer neglect and collapse) to attract list-buying clients are communication and service. Refresh your system with the following six checkpoints, a basic guide for increasing the profit potential of renting your list.

1. Review. When adding customers to your house file, make sure your service bureau or order-entry staff capture all possible information, and propose these selections to your list-renting clients. For internal reasons, you may not wish to, or may be prohibited from, offering all of your information. But each record should have most of the following:

- Recency of purchase
- Frequency of purchases
- Date of first purchase
- Date of last purchase
- Dollar amount of last purchase
- Cumulative dollar amount of all purchases
- Items (or at least item categories) purchased
- Method of payment (installment, check, COD, credit card)
- Source of name (rented list, space, TV)
- Personal information, when available (sex, age, income, title (Mr./Mrs./Ms.), business, home or new address, etc.)

2. Inform. Keep your clients, and all list brokers, frequently informed of changes, new developments and updated counts. Data cards, with all currently available information, should be prepared no less than twice annually. Mail special announcements between updates of the data cards, whenever a significant change in the list occurs. Some specifics to announce include:

- Frequency of updates
- Projections of counts (whenever possible)
- Changes in mailing patterns (new type offers, increase/decrease in outside list, TV, or space acquisition or disposal of a list source, etc.)
- Availability of new selection criteria

3. Contact. Face-to-face meetings and frequent phone contact enhance list rental income by building

comfortable relationships with brokers and clients. It's vital for keeping brokers' account executives aware of your list's "track record"; how and for whom it has been working, using what selection methods. These contacts help convince mailers to tell you specific results, even compare your list to others used. Recommending another test is more effective if offered personally, especially if your last rental did not work for the mailer.

4. Advertise. Attract new clients by making your list known to them. Your best proponent still is, of course, the list broker. But you can also stimulate new clients by advertising. Most probably will continue to place their orders through a broker, but advertising may catch their attention before a broker recommends you. Try advertising in trade journals, list directories, club newsletters, and meeting programs. Testing different advertising vehicles will help you determine where to advertise—and whether or not advertising works for you.

5. Follow-up. All list rentals should be tracked. Sixty to ninety days after the scheduled mail date, contact your broker to determine the client's results from mailing to your list. If the test was successful, suggest a commitment for a larger retest or a roll-out, and recommend testing additional segments of the list. If the list failed, try to find out which lists worked, and recommend segments of your file that, as closely as possible, resemble the successful lists.

6. Additional services. Your mailing list is only one source of list rental income. Others include:

- Package inserts: advertising material placed into your outgoing fulfillment packages
- Statement stuffers: advertising placed in your billing statements, if you offer credit terms
- Ride alongs: a statement stuffer included with your original direct mail package

- Co-op: several outside advertising pieces inserted by you into an envelope and mailed to your customers

☐

40. Avoid Unwise List Rentals

List rentals are highly profitable "extra" income producers, but maximizing list rental income does not mean accepting every order for your list. Some orders simply are unfit for your clients. It is true that customers who receive a mailing that is obscene, in bad taste, or a rip-off probably won't complain. They won't know that the offer came to them through your list rental. In fact, they probably won't even complain to the Better Business Bureau. What will happen is a lot worse. Your customer may reject direct mail advertising entirely and, in an effort to prevent his name from being rented, become an advocate of privacy legislation. If this happens often enough, the list business will be severely affected and that, in turn, will greatly reduce all direct-response marketing, including your own mailing efforts.

Responsible list owners read the sample mailing piece that comes with the list rental order. Does the offer sound legitimate? If there is any doubt, question the mailer. If necessary, ask for a sample of the product being offered. Make sure that your list has decoy names in it. Check to make sure that the sample submitted for clearance is the item actually mailed to your clients.

When checking out a new mailer's credit references, ask for some background information on the mailer himself. He may have been sued for non-delivery of merchandise, or forced to sign a cease and desist order from future advertising. Some years ago a $26 million suit was filed against a large list owner by people who were exposed to an allegedly fraudulent commodities options firm. The plaintiff's argument was that the list owner should have known the nature of the list renter's activities. This is an isolated case, but the only way to protect your customers, your list, and the future of list rentals from unscrupulous marketers is to check every rental request thoroughly.

□

CHAPTER FOUR

Choosing and Merchandising Products That Sell

ONE OF THE GREATEST CHALLENGES FACING CATALOG-ers is finding fresh, interesting merchandise to include in each book. If that challenge is not enough, the merchant must also look for special "hooks" to grab the customer's attention and get him or her to place an order.

The following chapter puts together the ideas you need to develop an effective merchandising plan.

☐

41. That All-Important First Impression: Handling Inquiries for Your Catalog

With increasing competition in virtually every merchandise segment of the catalog business, marketers have come to realize the critical need to continually attract new customers. But doing so on a cost-effective basis means more than just generating the inquiry, getting that name. The key is conversion. One of the most important catalogs or promotional packages you will ever send to a customer is that first one, your response to his or her inquiry. It's your introduction. It must present your company, products, services and guarantees, instill a credible, comfortable feeling in the customer and compel her to order. No small task, and there are an unlimited variety of ways to achieve it. To illustrate, we've focused on a hardworking inquiry response catalog package from Current, Inc. In response to inquiries, Current mails a

package of promotional material ranging from a small introductory brochure to its seasonal catalog. The lead-off piece is a four-page, folded 8¼″ × 5½″ brochure, a letter from Current founder Miriam Loo (Figure 27). Appropriately, the copy begins by thanking the customer for the inquiry. It then proceeds directly into a promotion of the catalog and the first of many benefits for the customer who shops with Current: "Quantity Discounts" on "group" orders. Pages two

Figure 27

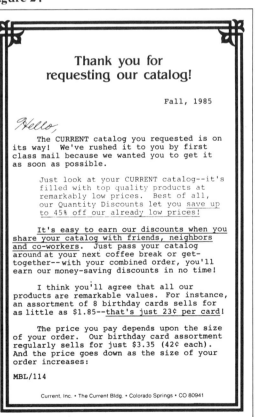

Figure 28

and three continue promoting discounts, inform the customer of free shipping for cash with order, comment on the company's quality products and service, state the guarantee and direct the customer to the catalog. There's even a "P.S." promoting Current products as fund-raising premiums. Page four presents a series of testimonials with name and city/state included.

The second element in the package, "Keeping Current," is a "newsletter" (four pages, full-color, 8¼" × 10½") that includes information on new products added to the Current line; a review of the greeting card printing process; a roster of personnel from the company; an article on things to do for kids, plus recipes and more testimonials (Figure 28). Page four presents sale merchandise and promotes a free gift offered for purchases over $50.

Next in line is a special full-color promotion titled "Fun for kids." Current bills it as "eight brand-new pages" of stickers, stationery products, cards and books for children. The promotion, designed like a catalog

signature, provides Current with a lot of latitude in presenting special sale merchandise, testing response to new products, or highlighting merchandise for a particular market (based on the source of the inquiry) or season. In numerous places in each of these promotions, customers are directed to the enclosed catalog (one of the company's sixty-four page seasonal books) and the catalog order form.

Current's order form is a separate six-page piece with an attached business reply envelope. The order form plays a pivotal role in tying together all of the "stuff" that comes out of this package. Current's form is complicated at first glance, but actually follows a logical sequence. First, it reviews discounts, free gift, guarantee policy, price guarantees and merchandise availability. Then it proceeds with a stepwise procedure for ordering items from each of the promotional pieces. The final section of the order form contains space to fill out an order summary, for providing a daytime phone number and for providing payment information. Last but not least, Current uses a panel on the BRE to promote a surprise package ($20.00 worth of merchandise for $6.95), and goes out selling.

Merchandise selection and pricing aside, in designing this inquiry-response package, it appears that Current has taken the time to evaluate all of the reasons customers might have for *not* placing an order, and how to use every square inch of space either for presenting merchandise or building company credibility and trust . . . or both. This first impression is critical to getting that first order. Quality product, service and effective marketing create the repeat customer. But the inquiry-response promotion turns prospects into new customers. Evaluate your "first impression" package. You may find it's not working as hard as it could.

42. How to Find New Products and New Suppliers without Attending Trade Shows

You don't have to spend all your time and money traveling to merchandise trade shows in search of new products and suppliers. Though shows are prime hunting grounds for products, costs for travel, hotels and restaurants add up to a hefty total. Because many companies can afford to attend only one or two shows a year, an attempt is made to choose the most productive shows. But even the best will not produce enough products or sources to keep a catalog business healthy and thriving year-round. And even if you attend many shows, you still will not find the number of products you really need, nor will you have all your product-searching opportunities covered.

What do you do, especially if you wish to find good, new products at a reasonable cost? There are several productive avenues to take, but one of the most rewarding and least expensive is found while sitting behind your desk. A constant flow of new products and suppliers comes from three "behind the desk" sources of merchandise supply:

- competitors' catalogs
- magazines and newspapers
- your own mail and phone

Don't underrate the importance of a "competitor research" program. Analyze competitors' catalogs to determine which categories of products are selling, which specific products move well, and the time of year these products are strong sellers. Though the object of this program is to learn what sells well for your competition, another rewarding aspect of the analysis is that it provides a convenient avenue for finding new product manufacturers and sources. After all, not *all* excellent products are available from supply sources that attend shows; some sources for these products may be "mysteries" to you. But if you see the item in a competitor's catalog, you have a good chance of discovering the source: just order the product. When it arrives, it's usually accompanied by the manufacturer's name and address. Frequently this information is printed on the box containing the product, on a label, a set of instructions, or even molded into the product itself. Now you can contact the manufacturer directly. At the very least, you may find that an imported product lists only the country of origin. In this case, your next step is to contact your current suppliers of imported goods. If they don't already have the item in their lines, chances are they can find out where and how to get it for you.

Other fruitful new product sources can be found in the mail-order advertising sections of magazines and newspapers. Look in the back of general consumer magazines first (where most of the mail-order ads are), so your concentration is at its peak. *House Beautiful, Better Homes & Gardens* and *Seventeen* have good mail-order sections, and regional magazines like *Yankee, Sunset* and *Southern Living* have some of the most powerful mail-order advertising sections. Try the *Los Angeles Times, Chicago Tribune,* the *New York Times Magazine* and the *Christian Science Monitor.* More specialized merchandise lines do well in specialized magazines. For sports equipment and clothing, good sources are *Field & Stream, Sports Afield* and *Outdoor Life.* Wedding and entertainment products can be found in *Brides Magazine, Modern Bride* and *Metropolitan Home.* For electronics and auto items, read *Popular Mechanics Monthly, Road & Track* and *Car & Driver.* Watch for products that are repeated by competitors, so you'll know the items are successful. Order them, and then contact the manufacturer to investigate running the product in your catalog.

Perhaps the most overlooked "behind the desk" opportunity is your own mail. It's easy to toss it in your wastebasket or have someone else sort it, throwing away the advertising. Don't. Take time to look at each piece. This advertising literature provides a wonderful opportunity to find a prized "needle in the haystack" and requires little time or expense. Also, look at letters received from individuals. Many include actual samples or amateurish snapshots of proposed products. Use your experience and intuition to sort out the winners. And don't ignore phone calls. A few minutes of conversation can produce a winner, too.

These methods of new product research may seem less interesting than traveling to trade shows, but they pay high dividends and are a lot easier on the feet. Just a couple of hours a week devoted to this type of buying trip will produce a steady source of winning products.

Lou Smith, President, Lou E. Smith Associates

□

43. Magazines and Newspapers: A Terrific Resource for New Item Searches

Publications with sections in which many companies advertise products for sale by mail feature two types of ads that should be of particular interest to you. Mail-order companies advertise because they want to acquire new names to whom they can send their catalogs or brochures. For their ads, they choose strong items from their product line, knowing that the buyers they attract will fit their present image (customer profile) and help build their main customer list. Finding single product ads repeated by a small manufacturer are like finding pure gold. In most cases the manufacturer who runs a product ad time and again is not looking for names, because it has no catalog to mail. It has a product that is selling, one that makes money when advertised in consumer publications.

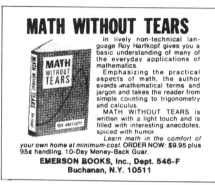

Figure 29

Five points you should look for in magazines and newspaper ads are

1. Visual Presentation. Does the product photograph well? Can you tell what it is or what it does at first glance?

2. Product Benefit. Is it obvious? Does the picture or headline immediately show the benefit?

3. Ad Repetition. Has the ad appeared in a monthly publicaton every month, or at least four times in a year . . . in a weekly, once every four weeks or more . . . in a daily, three to four times a month?

4. Multi Media. Has the ad appeared in several different magazines or newspapers? Has it appeared in both magazines and newspapers?

5. Your Catalog Image. Does the product fit your image? Is the product similar to or in the same price range as your products?

When you are examining potential products in magazine and newspaper ads, you should consider these five points:

1. Visual Presentation is good. The book is photogenic and its title is a headline, a plus when shown in limited catalog space.

2. Product Benefits jumps out at you: no more frustration with math! More subtle benefits are suggested in the last sentence: Learn math at low cost in the privacy and convenience of your home. Purchase

the vehicle to do so by mail, so you avoid the embarrassment of broadcasting your shortcoming.

3. Ad Repetition is proven because "Math Without Tears" is in every '81 issue of *Yankee* magazine, a prolific mail-order publication.

4. Multi Media is secure. From September through December 1981, "Math Without Tears" ran at least fourteen times in *The Wall Street Journal.* That meets the multi media requirement nicely.

5. Your Catalog Image. This requirement can be judged only by you. If this product fits, get in touch with the publisher. You may have found a winner for your catalog!

☐

44. Visualization of Art and Copy: A Valuable Exercise When Considering Products for Your Catalog

When your merchandise buyers are searching for new products, they should consider the "appropriateness" of given products for sale through your catalog. How effectively can they be portrayed and promoted in art and copy? Your merchandising staff should incorporate the following two steps in their evaluation of each product.

1. Art visualization. Look at the product, visualize how it will appear in the catalog, and ask the following questions. Will the product photograph well? Will its benefits appear readily enough to entice the customer to read the copy? Does your photographer have the skill to photograph it properly? Can the product be photographed so that all details and features are clearly portrayed? Without essential details, the product may have little appeal and sales will die.

Consider presenting the item in one or more line drawings, including "exploded" or action insets, or don't list it.

As a merchandiser, you must select products which will sell well in your catalog. Part of selling is the ability to visually entice the customer to buy. A merchandiser who is able to visualize how the product will look in the catalog will be able to assist your photography, design and copy staff in effectively presenting the product. Your merchandisers must visualize art for the product in the context of your catalog, its image, and the other products it includes.

2. Copy headline visualization. Can you imagine how the headline for a given product will read? Often when you are looking at an item, headlines will pop into your mind, possibly because of a need the product fills or because of its multiple uses. What are the benefits of the product? A good merchandiser is trained to look for the benefits that a product will give your customer. Those benefits are best used as the bases of headlines and promotional copy. When looking at a desk which includes a modular work station and typing wing, you might think, "Here's an all-in-one-work area." Or when you are examining a calculator that figures the number of calories your body burns, you might think, "It's a little computer for losing weight."

When selecting items for your catalog, write down your thoughts and impressions of each. Go over the customer benefits and product advantages with your creative people. Isn't thinking about art and headlines the creative department's job? Yes—but the more information you can give them about why you selected the item and the feelings you had while selecting it, the better the job they can do.

☐

45. Take Some of the Guesswork Out of Choosing New Items for Your Catalog

Instinct and personal taste reflected in the choice of an item have started many catalog programs. Bill Nicolai of Early Winters began with a unique tent that he constructed himself. Lillian Katz started what is today the Lillian Vernon Corporation with monogrammed belts and purses in a space ad. These entrepreneurs, like many others, began with instinct, personal taste and what they sensed was a marketable item.

Mail order companies do not begin with great ideas for graphics or copywriting. They start with merchandise. The art and copy promote and support that merchandise (and can make or break it). But the item comes first. Merchandise will always be the basis of your business. Without it, you've got nothing to sell, no matter how good your presentation techniques are.

But even though instinct and a good idea may have initiated the first item offered by a mail order business, those qualities cannot be the sole, continued support. Every item cannot be successfully chosen by "feelings," and good ideas are hard to come by continually. So what does one do?

At the risk of removing the romance from mail order merchandising, here's one answer. Look at your success, and try to *analyze* (forget instinct now) its origin. Bill Nicolai may have decided to build his business on quality construction and unique designs that solved outdoor problems well—and Lillian Katz may have felt that personalization was a key element to selling quality accessories at reasonable prices.

Never forget that the product and those who respond to it become a team—like peaches and cream. As soon as you develop a sales response, you develop

customer expectations to fill "like" needs. So the place to start when choosing new items is with your own line. Begin by analyzing it.

1. What is the percentage of product mix? How many kitchen items do you carry? How many tools, ladies' accessories, household decorations? Place items into categories and see what percentage of the total items presented each category contains.

2. In each category, compare the percentages of items which sell outstandingly well to those which are average or poor sellers.

Point 1 of the above analysis will tell you, for example, that your line consists of 40% kitchen items, 10% tools, 30% ladies' accessories and 20% decorative gifts. Point 2 will tell you that 50% of your kitchen items are above-average sellers, 30% are average, and 20% are poor. If only 10% of the decorative gifts are above average, with 60% average and 30% poor, you now can draw some conclusions. Kitchen items have an excellent chance of success in your book, and the category can be expanded. Decorative items sell less well and too many new entries in that area become risky.

Trends can be sensed within each category as well. If a tart maker, a radish rosebudder and a cake decorating kit consistently outsell the cheese grater and the toaster tongs, your customers may be looking to you for kitchen items that help them make "fancy" foods. So when choosing to list either a set of mixing bowls or a french bean slicer, you can predict that the slicer, although not a guaranteed success, is more likely to be a good seller.

So the first area of your concern when selecting new items is determining which old items sell well, and why. You're trying to shift the odds to get a better chance of making the right decision.

When you begin to see the trends, you can develop a "formula" for new items. You'll get an idea of how many new entries should be presented in each book, and how many should fall in each category. If your catalog has space to present 100 items, perhaps you'll discover that approximately 15 percent should be new. And of those fifteen new items, you may discover that seven should be kitchen items, three should be ladies' accessories, three should be tools, and two should be decorative items.

If you publish four catalogs a year, you will have to compare book-for-book, as you may find seasonal variations in your customers' responses. Even if your catalog is a specialty book that presents only tools, you'll find that this analysis holds. Rasps may be stronger than screwdrivers. Lathes may sell strongly at Christmas, but poorly in summer.

The issue of merchandise selection is not pat and not "scientific." It is a combination of analysis of "knowns" upon which you build with instinct and creative thinking. And don't forget that the catalog business is a job of repeat selling: enticing new customers to make their first purchase, luring the customer to purchase again. If you don't have the right products for your customer list, plus a constant supply of viable new products, you may be doomed to failure.

Preparing to be a success in this weighty field of item selection involves discipline: research and analysis through systematic record keeping. Creativity and natural ability help, but they cannot sustain a continuous selection of successful merchandise. You need a good, solid research program. And to follow up on this research, you need to get your hands on catalogs from every supplier of the type of merchandise you'll carry. You must attend trade shows and nose around merchandise marts.

Check competitors' catalogs to find products that are selling. Discover which products are on thir way out. Find new suppliers. Set up competitive pricing. You also can find data on order form design, shipping charges, general policies, art/copy formats.

Check magazines and newspapers to find new products. Find new suppliers. Find the competition's hottest selling items.

Analyze your own catalog sales to see what product categories sell best for you: what time of year is best for specific products; how to stretch a product's selling period; where to place products to increase sales.

Analyze your returns to see what causes an item to be unsatisfactory. Find out if merchandise breaks in shipping. Discover if items are shoddy, incorrectly sized.

Listen to your customers. Your customer service department can pass on suggestions received from customers for products you do not carry. Customers will also tell you if you have a catalog art, photo or copy error (which usually harms sales).

Follow this research program and you won't have to guess about good items. You'll have some of the information needed to sustain a successful merchandising process year after year.

☐

46. How to Determine What Your Customer Wants to Buy: Establishing a Customer Preference Guide through Individual Product Sales

The most important aspect of merchandise selection is knowing what your customer wants. The best way to establish this is to look at catalog sales history in each product category. The most accurate approach is to compare catalog products in terms of *sales per square inch*. To have an assessment you can manage, first evaluate categories.

For instance, a kitchen supplies catalog might break its product line into the following categories:

- Serving pieces—plates and platters, bowls, silverware, cups and glasses
- Cutlery—carving knives, paring knives, cutting blocks and boards, shears and cleavers
- Cookware and appliances—toasters, mixers, baking dishes, pots and pans
- Kitchen paraphernalia—timers, potholders, dishtowels, spice racks
- Food processing equipment—blenders, dehydrators, yogurt/ice cream makers, juicers

Once product categories are established, calculate total dollar sales derived from each category. Then calculate total square inches devoted to each category of products in the catalog and equate into dollars per square inch. Then appraise the categories according to ranking by dollars per square inch.

For example, the kitchen supplies categories might break out like this.

Category	Total square inches	Total dollars	Dollars per square inch
Cookware and appliances	600	25,000	41.60
Cutlery	200	8,000	40.00
Serving pieces	800	30,000	37.50
Kitchen paraphernalia	500	16,000	32.00
Food processing equipment	400	10,000	25.00

You have established your customer preference guide. Note that the order of preference is established by the greatest amount of dollars per square inch, not the largest amount of square inches devoted to a category or the greatest amount of total dollar sales per category. Customer preference is established by how well the product category performs in relation to the space devoted to it. To further refine this preference guide, study the products and their sales within each category.

Cookware and Appliances

Product type	Total square inches	Total dollars	Dollars per square inch
Toasters	110	6,000	54.55
Mixers	95	4,000	42.11
Baking dishes			
casserole	60	3,000	50.00
cake	60	2,000	33.33
Pots and pans			
cake pans	70	2,000	28.57
kettles	40	1,000	25.00
frying pans	95	4,000	42.11
saucepans	70	3,000	42.86

This hypothetical study shows the three most popular products within the cookware/appliances category are toasters, casserole dishes and saucepans. Expanding the number of products in these subcategories, and the number of square inches devoted, should produce the greatest increase in sales. Two other subcategories should be looked at carefully—cake pans and kettles. The customer preference study shows demand is low. Perhaps you should include fewer items in these categories and devote less space to these products, as they produce the fewest sales for the space alloted.

☐

47. A Product Information Form: What Is It, and Why Do You Need One?

You've found a product and a source of supply, but you need plenty of questions answered before you can list it. You'll need information for art and copy production, for retail pricing, for purchasing, and for warehousing. You need a Product Information Form asking about the following items:

1. The supplier 1. Company name, address, phone
    2. Person to contact, title
    3. Area marketing rep, phone
    4. Credit references

Tip: Large companies have regional, state or local representatives you can deal with—but you may realize a greater discount if you deal directly with the company. A rep can help with delivery problems.

2. The product 1. Stock number, name of product
    2. Country of origin
    3. Dimensions, inches, ounces
    4. Materials: wood, metal, etc.
    5. Intrinsic details, such as UL listing, battery-operated, etc.
    6. Sizes and colors available; percent of sales in each category

Tip: The stock number is the key for suppliers' processing; use it for speedier transactions. An import may need to be ordered early. Materials and components are essential for catalog description. Knowing the mix of percent of sales helps you project quantity needs and decide which colors to list (drop the low sellers).

3. Pricing and drop shipping 1. Recommended retail
    2. Cost each; quantity cost breaks
    3. Is product pre-priced? Dollar amount?
    4. How about a "guaranteed sales" deal?
    5. Is drop shipping available? At what cost?

Tip: The supplier may consider total quantity ordered during the life of your catalog for quantity discounts—ask! Pre-pricing can be a problem; see if it can be deleted. You can avoid overstock with "guaranteed sales," but the product will cost more. When the supplier drop-ships to your customer, you save costs of warehousing, freight and overstock.

4. Packaging 1. Master shipping carton quantity
    2. Weight of master carton
    3. Individual packaging: display, bulk, poly bag, individual mailer

Tip: Suppliers prefer shipping full cartons; if shipping less, costs may be higher. Display packaging crushes easily when mailed; a poly bag is less costly and may work as well.

5. Shipping and terms 1. FOB point
    2. Shipping point
    3. Payment terms
    4. Freight allowance

Tip: Who pays the freight? Will terms or allowances help keep your costs down?

6. Availability 1. Is it in stock; if not, when?
    2. Is supply continuous, or are there seasonal lows?
    3. What is normal on-hand supply?
    4. How long will it take to ship after receipt of order?

Tip: Be sure the product is actually manufactured and in stock before cataloging. If you don't, you may find yourself refunding all orders.

7. Advertising and production

1. How many samples do you want?

2. How about a glossy photo or transparency?

3. Any supplier contributions toward cost of art and copy?

4. Any advertising allowances?

Tip: Get enough samples for evaluation, testing, art, and copy. If you are cataloging plants or food, the manufacturer may have a transparency you'll want to use. Many will contribute to photography costs. Some will pay an advertising allowance upon proof of publication. Ask.

---

8. Product sales experience

1. Any previous sales in mail order, and with whom? (Ask for a clipping.)

2. If sold in media, ask for a copy of advertisements.

3. Ask for company sales literature.

Tip: Never miss a chance to see how the product has been previously presented. Get as much sales history as you can. Art and copy samples will help produce your catalog presentation.

Miscellaneous Tips: Ask about other items offered by the company; don't ever miss a chance to find new items. State your mail-order status on the form to indicate your need for jobber discounts and price protections once an item is cataloged. Ask about product warranty protection on defective merchandise. Bonafide sources will tell you the *amount of liability they carry. Use this if needed; it will keep your own insurance payments down. Finally, allow a space for the signature of an officer of the source company; it's more binding than a rep's.*

☐

48. How to Work with Small Suppliers

Just like people who started mail-order businesses at their kitchen tables, many suppliers or manufacturers start businesses in their garages. "Garage suppliers" may be homemakers, moonlighters or students who are woodworking or sewing in the garage, basement or family room. Many are starting in business for the first time and don't know much about supplying merchandise for a catalog operation.

Extra effort and consideration needs to be given to this type of supplier. Why bother? Because some of the best products you find may be from garage suppliers. Don't be afraid of them: with your help and guidance, they can become good sources.

Don't expect the garage supplier to be familiar with the jargon and terms used in mail order. Explain your price and mark-up requirements and volume needs. These will come as a surprise. Mark-ups needed in mail order typically are less than retail mark-ups but greater than generally realized. And, depending on your company size, your volume could seem disappointing or overwhelming. Once the garage supplier understands your mark-up and volume needs, he or she will ask other questions. The five most common are answered here.

1. Q. Will you pay for the products in advance?

A. No. Make no exceptions. If suppliers need financing, let them go to the bank, friends or relatives. If you do not hold fast to this rule, you'll risk losing your funds if suppliers cannot fulfill production promises.

2. Q. Can large orders be filled in increments?

A. Yes. Be sure you state suggested delivery dates well in advance, and place your order well ahead of time. State when your total order must be in your warehouse.

3. Q. Should additional supply be manufactured in the beginning?

A. No. But the supplier must be prepared to provide additional products quickly upon notification. Take special care with projections. The garage supplier will be on a tight budget. Go over your ordering needs step by step and be sure to follow up, informing the supplier of any increase or decrease in needs. Announce relisting intentions and needs early!

4. Q. Is fancy packaging required?

A. Your answer depends on your image. If you are a high-ticket gift catalog, you may need fancier packaging than a low-ticket general merchandise catalog. To help the garage supplier in the beginning, you may be able to go with a poly bag or plain carton. If the product proves to be a fantastic seller, the extra cost and trouble of fancier packaging may be justified. Remember, the customer is purchasing the product shown in your catalog artwork, not the packaging.

5. Q. Should a patent or copyright be applied for?

A. Encourage the garage supplier to question a lawyer closely about the protection provided by these legal devices, and about how easy it may be for competitors to get around this protection.

Your garage suppliers are sure to ask about these three areas of referral at one time or another.

1. Who can supply raw material wholesale? Some garage suppliers begin by purchasing their raw material and supplies at the retail level and do not know where else to find supply. You already know, or can easily find out, where to purchase dowels, wood, metals, nuts and bolts, etc., in volume and at a lower price, helping your cost to be lower too.

2. Who might be interested in manufacturing the product? Perhaps the actual manufacturing becomes too much for the garage supplier, who turns to you for a manufacturing reference. Suggest a good manufacturer of plastics, tubing, printing or whatever field is needed. Remember, the new manufacturer will be your supplier in the future.

3. Where can a product representative be found? The garage supplier who wants to expand (and is able to) will require the help of a good sales rep. The supplier is likely to ask if you know one. Recommend reps who have served you well and have represented product lines well. Do not promise that your supplier's product will be accepted.

☐

49. How to Handle Product Suppliers When They Consistently Miss Delivery Dates

There are three ways merchandisers can plan ahead to avoid problems when suppliers are late delivering goods to your warehouse.

First, notify the supplier in advance that you are listing the product. Then project the number of units needed per product, and tell the supplier. Finally, you should find an alternate source of supply for each product you list. Depending upon the number of products you list in your catalog, the first two actions can be handled manually or automatically accomplished by your computer.

Now, suppose you observe these plan-ahead actions. What can be done when a supplier continues to give poor delivery, continues to miss promised delivery dates?

First of all, *discuss the problem*—first with the company representative, then with the company President, if necessary. If you happen to own stock in the company, write the Chairman of the Board. You're guaranteed to see fast action! Make sure you clearly explain the cost consequences you are suffering: customer orders placed on back order easily cost $5 or more for processing and handling. Having to split a customer's order to send the back-ordered item at a later date makes processing and packaging cost twice as much. Postage can double, too. In addition, increased customer complaints place an additional load on your Customer Service Department, and most importantly, customers become unhappy! Informing the supplier of these extra costs can be most beneficial when negotiating an equitable solution.

Request that products be shipped by air at the supplier's expense! Figure the cost difference between normal methods of delivery and air delivery and ask the supplier to pay the difference. After all, the delay is costing you money and customer satisfaction, so it is only fair that the supplier share some of the consequences—especially if you have planned ahead and given plenty of notice.

Request payment for customer notification of delayed shipment. Law requires you to notify customers if the products they have ordered are going to be delayed in shipment for thirty days or more. Separate notification must be given many times and costs a minimum of 15 cents for postage and another 5 to 10 cents for printing a double postcard to notify and provide customers with a return response vehicle.

Ask the supplier to find you extra goods from another customer or another source. Many times a competitor has extra stock that can be shared until your shipment arrives and can be replaced in time for their use (your competitors won't mind helping you if they know that turn-about is fair play). Suppliers are always aware of their competitors and the goods they carry, can usually order from them easily. Or, if your supplier's relationship with competitors is poor, your source can at least tell you of another source, and you can negotiate a temporary supply. A smart supplier knows that any way he helps you to maintain your inventory will keep you on his side.

Inform the supplier of your intention to change sources. If you have tried every way of working out your problems with your current supplier and you have planned well by lining up alternate suppliers, lay it on the line: give realistic delivery dates and adhere to them or you will change sources. If you do not have an alternate supplier because the product is unique, try finding a very similar product or a manufacturer interested in making one. (Remember that your volume needs must be substantial to justify a new manufacturer setting up for a product it is not presently manufacturing.) If none of these alternatives is workable, you must drop the product from your line, no matter how well it sells. If it can't be shipped promptly, your costs will become too high, your profits will disappear, your customers will become unhappy, and you will lose them.

□

50. For a Smooth Operation, Evaluate Your Supplier's Performance at Least Once a Year

Finding a product, initiating supply and analyzing results is not the end of the merchandiser's responsibility. Continued consideration must be given to the quality of service the supplier provides. Though new suppliers may cause problems because they must become accustomed to your needs and demands, they are not the only ones about whom you should be concerned. Suppliers you have dealt with for years need to be evaluated, too. Three areas need formal evaluation at least once a year.

1. Delivery. How well has the supplier met your delivery dates? How many purchase orders have been or are outstanding, and for how long? Assess these two different types:

a. Regular purchase orders. These are orders you've placed which allow a reasonable or normal lead time for delivery. This may be six weeks to three months or even longer, depending on the type of product or component being ordered and the type of supplier. If a product is being manufactured just for you, the manufacturer will need a longer lead time to plan raw material and production needs. Also, imported products normally take longer to supply simply because of delivery distance. If the product is common to the market, mass production will make the lead time shorter.

If the supplier has had few delays in this area in the past year, you have no need for concern. But if there have been consistent delays on regular purchase orders, it's time to talk with the supplier to ascertain why. It's important for your source of supply to realize that delayed shipments cause you the extra expense of informing customers of the delay. You're also bearing the brunt of issuing refunds and losing profits you could have gained if a fulfillable item had been cataloged instead. Your customers are unhappy and your company credibility suffers.

b. Urgent purchase orders. These include orders with short lead time which you've issued because of unpredictable sales. New products often fall into this category because the response to them is unknown. If sales take off rapidly, you may have to phone in additional orders until you can estimate the sales demand.

Space ads also can produce large quantity demands which were not initially predictable.

If the supplier has failed to come through for you on a reasonable number of urgent orders, you need to know why. A good source of supply will "pull out the stops" when needed. Unforeseen quantity demands cannot always be filled immediately, but if the supplier can't handle a good number of them, his system or his attitude is faulty. You may have to consider a different source of supply. Make it a matter of course to find second or third sources on as many items in your catalog as possible. Their value is seen when your usual source cannot fill your needs.

2. Product Quality. Has the quality of the product and its packaging retained the same standards it exhibited when it was first cataloged? It should be maintained at this level, or improved. If a problem such as breakage, omitted components, or faulty product instructions has developed, how quickly and satisfactorily has the supplier reacted? If you have arranged for the supplier to replace customer refund units, has he honored his agreement? Problems which are not taken care of in a reasonable amount of time need your attention.

3. Price. Has your volume usage gone up from what was initially planned and negotiated? If so, maybe you should renegotiate for a better price. Are competitors able to sell the product for less than you? Ask your supplier for a lower cost. Do you have acceptable alternate sources who will give you a low enough price to justify switching suppliers?

When your analysis is complete, list the problem suppliers and evaluate their importance to your company. Do they supply products critical to your business, or just marginal listings? Do you have alternate sources who could satisfactorily supply your company? Contact your current supplier to see if you can work problems out. Even a "problem assessment" visit to the plants of major suppliers may be warranted. Make every effort to work things out because good products and good suppliers are hard to find. Establish and maintain an honest interchange with your supplier if you wish him to be a good source. He must know your needs, and vice versa. A relationship of this type with your supplier is healthy.

Once an evaluation has been made and problems have been met head-on, keep an eye on performance. Initiate a follow-up program to ensure that you receive continued good service. Analyses and evaluations such as these will help the merchandiser understand and deal with the problems of reordering, inventory and customer refunds. And it will make the company more profitable, too.

Lou Smith, President, Lou E. Smith Associates

☐

51. Drop Shipping: What Is It?

Arranging to have the supplier or manufacturer ship the item directly to your customer (rather than to your warehouse) is drop shipping. You provide the supplier with ordering information (which item, how many, how should it be personalized, etc.) plus a shipping label pre-printed with your customer's name and address. The return address on the label is yours . . . not the supplier's.

When to use drop shipping

Generally, the cataloger asks for drop-shipping services only when he has to, because fulfillment time is lost in sending instructions to the drop shipper, and control is lost in expediting the order from someplace besides the cataloger's own location. But sometimes the nature of the item makes drop shipping the only practical solution.

1. Perishable Items.
   a. Nursery products. Most plants and seeds need (or benefit from) climatically-controlled storage. Some nursery products fall under government regulations that require close monitoring.

   b. Food. Packaging can be complicated. Storage situations, usually refrigeration, must be maintained to avoid spoilage. Chocolate, for example, can be sent only at certain seasons.

2. Personalized Items. A cataloger without metal engravers, printing presses, or hand lettering facilities must have an outside source in order to personalize his listings of jewelry, stationery, etc.

3. Over-sized Items. Extra large or excessively heavy items may use too much of the cataloger's warehouse space. These items may have to be shipped by rail to the customer. It's unrealistic and costly to bring heavy items in-house, and re-ship to the customer.

4. Live Items. Chickens, ants, earthworms, lady bugs, etc., must be shipped by the originator. Individual state and federal regulations must be followed closely or sales will be stopped.

5. New Items. Test sales strength before committing to a large inventory on an untried item.

Not all suppliers will drop ship. Planning to have all the items in your catalog drop shipped automatically limits your selection. There are many advantages to drop shipping, such as delayed cash outlay and little capital risk, but the disadvantages are plentiful, too.

☐

52. Calling Attention to Product Detail: When Does It Pay?

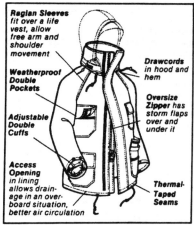

Figure 30

Almost every product has details that are important but subsidiary to its main features. These main features, which can be quite simple, can be shown easily in a straight, one-product-shot approach. But sometimes the catalog marketer must show the product with more than one shot, or call attention to extra details using line drawings instead of photography. Here are three instances in which extra details should be illustrated.

1. Construction of Product. When a product is constructed with unusual techniques that cannot be seen immediately, it may require a second shot or a line drawing. Example: a fireproof safe with an unusual inner wall construction, or the GTX Foul Weather Jacket from Eddie Bauer. This line drawing inset shows seven details of exceptional quality added to an already acceptable weather-fighting piece of clothing. The raglan sleeves fit easy over bulky clothing, pockets are weatherproof, double cuffs keep out the wind, access opening at bottom allows drainage in an "overboard" situation (plus good air circulation), drawcords promote snug, warm fit, and the oversized zipper is guarded by storm flaps. An ordinary photograph of this jacket obviously would show it as heavy-duty, cold weather apparel. But would it sell as well without the added incentive given by the unusual details shown in the "second shot"?

2. Secondary Benefits. When a product's auxiliary benefits carry its functions beyond those of an ordinary item, it is usually necessary to spotlight those benefits separately. Day-Timer's business supply catalog sells calendars with benefits that are additional to a calendar's basic function. Figure 31 shows five secondary benefits of their monthly Wall Calendar: (1) a

Figure 31

separate reference page for phone numbers, (2) future month reference, (3) construction that allows easy discard of old months, (4) room for individual daily notes, and (5) custom personalization. The lines in the illustration are "pointers" from explanatory copy. These secondary benefits give the product more appeal for the business person and consequently build sales.

3. Extra Service. Sometimes the benefit which the customer needs to see is not connected to a single product but to an entire product line. Art Poster Company sells art posters at affordable prices, allowing customers to enjoy artwork by grand masters and

innovative newcomers. But they also offer skillful custom framing. The two center pages of their catalog are devoted to describing the type and quality of the frames and the care taken in framing and shipping the print to the customer. The catalog includes a nine-step visual that highlights the process. These nine carefully illustrated steps encourage the customer to take advantage of the framing service, and increase the size of the average order for Art Poster Company.

These illustrations have called attention to product detail for one major reason: to generate additional sales. Be sure to look for opportunities to merchandise the extra details in your product line, too. It's an excellent way to build sales!

□

Your Feet Deserve the Best

Yes...Wright shoes are well made. But more important is how well they take care of your feet! As you walk, each foot bears the full weight of your body. <u>Each foot has three main arches,</u> placed to <u>hold the body weight</u>...<u>to brace your foot</u>...to <u>give support and strength</u> to what would otherwise be a weak and delicate arrangement of bones and muscles.

WRIGHT ARCH PRESERVER SHOES protect and support these arches with an insole that is molded under heat and high pressure. The result is not only strength, but a degree of comfort that is simply not experienced in ordinary shoes.

Figure 32

Use **Burpee's Easy-Sow Straight-Row Seed Tapes.** Easier to plant, precisely spaced seeds reduce thinning, encourage uniform growth. (See page 76.)

Figure 33

53. Product Education: A Clever Merchandising Approach That Brings in Dollars

The more difficult the product is to sell, the greater the payoff for educating the customer! Two basic ways to approach product education are education with the product copy and education individually highlighted within the catalog. Techniques used to make this education interesting almost always combine copy and art.

Two difficult-to-sell product categories in the general consumer area are shoes and seeds: shoes because of size variance among manufacturers and the importance of a good fit; seeds because they are readily available in retail stores at highly competitive prices.

Executive Shoes' catalog, Wright Arch Preserver Shoes, devotes one full catalog page to educating the customer about its shoe manufacturing process. Figure 32 shows a portion of this page, which tells about foot structure and relates how Wright Arch Preserver Shoes accommodate the foot's functions. This copy is supported by photographs of craftsmen involved in the shoe-manufacturing process.

Burpee's seed catalog educates the customer throughout the book with small art and copy blocks. Figure 33 uses just a few words to educate the consumer about seed planting while selling a product line and referring the customer to another part of the catalog. This marvelous little blurb is used on four different pages of the catalog. In addition, Burpee uses a two-page chart to recommend various plants for short borders, tall backgrounds, and rock gardens, discussing the best time of year to sow and whether the plants need sun or shade. The consumer cannot help but feel

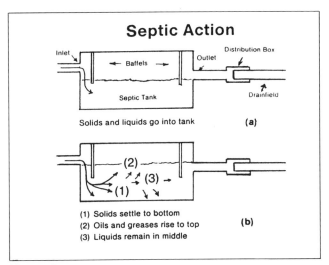

Figure 34

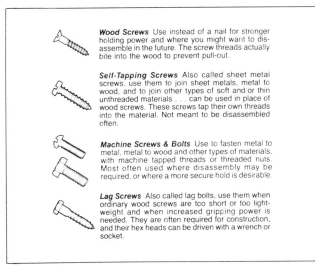

Figure 35

that Burpee offers the easiest way possible to plant a garden—a feeling Burpee has cultivated through product education, something not available with "rack" seeds.

Smart business catalogs educate consumers also. Brown Deer Co., Inc., a concentrated chemical catalog, devotes an entire page to septic tank care, com-

bining art diagrams and copy to educate its customers. Figure 34 is a portion of a diagram showing how liquid passes through a septic tank system. Extensive copy explains this flow and identifies some typical problems and how they can be avoided. The opposite page is devoted to a product, sold in the catalog, which solves septic tank problems. The education continues on the next page, where related products are illustrated and sold.

The half page DRI Industries devotes to its "Guide to Selection and Use of Fasteners" tells what to consider before starting a project involving fasteners and educates the customer with illustrations showing the six basic fasteners. Figure 35 identifies various styles using line drawings matched to copy describing individual usage. Two following catalog pages sell a large variety of fasteners.

Each of these examples skillfully "educates" the consumer into buying. If you have a difficult or overly common product line, consider educating your customer. The easier-to-sell, glamour products also benefit from product education.

□

54. Tell Your Customer about Your Exclusive Products

Buyers search for unique products to call their own: products which they have the exclusive right to sell by mail, or original products developed and manufactured for their catalog only. Many companies become known for having unique merchandise not

DON'T MISS OUR
CHESAPEAKE BAY TRADING CO.
EXCLUSIVES. LOOK FOR THE

Figure 36-A

**PARK SEEDS are High Performers™
in Your Garden because . . .**
One dominant goal governs our every endeavor: to develop and
offer better varieties bred for your home garden and delivered by
fast, convenient service to your doorstep. You'll get vegetables
with better taste and higher yield; flowers more beautiful and
easier to grow. We know you will, because we garden-test
thousands of varieties so those we endorse will perform in your
garden more successfully. Don't jeopardize your gardening
pleasure, use Park Seeds . . . they're proven **High Performers™**.
Look for the symbol **HP**, your sign of success and satisfaction—special selected **High Performer™** vegetable
and flower varieties are the cream of the crop! We highly
recommend these as being the easiest to grow and most widely
adapted. **HP** vegetables consistently have superior flavor,
heavier yield and a longer bearing period. **HP** flowers bloom
earlier, more profusely, with better colors and improved garden
habit. Grow a really great garden this year, start with **High
Performers™**.

Figure 36-B

found elsewhere by mail. Exclusivity is attractive not
only because the products are unique, but also because
an exclusive product is a good selling tool. But the
cataloger must tell the customer that this product is
exclusive! Not to do so would defeat the purpose of
exclusivity, and a valuable sales tool would go unused.

Here is how three companies let customers know
about their exclusive products.

1. Chesapeake Bay Trading Company's clothing
catalog (Figure 36) grabs the customer's attention
with an announcement identifying a special symbol.
It tells the customer about exclusives on the outside
back cover of the catalog wrap-around. The back cover positioning of this announcement is a prime reading
spot; it will not be missed. The symbol is placed within the product art of those listings which enjoy exclusivity to help the aware customer look for products
bearing this special distinction.

2. In its letter from the president (page two),
Papillon announces that it has "Some of the best
shopping anywhere, with many items exclusive to,
and available only through, Papillon." To identify
these special items within the catalog, a banner stating "exclusively ours" spans the photo. The "exclusive" banner is a fine attention-getter that makes the
product even more noteworthy.

3. The Park Seeds catalog really lets its customers know about special "High Performers"—seeds
which are exclusively Park's. Figure 36-B shows the
copy that explains "High Performers" and the symbol
that identifies these seeds throughout the catalog.
The bright red and yellow symbol is placed on product
photos throughout the catalog. The customer's eye is
immediately drawn to the product.

By telling the customer about product exclusives
and calling attention to those exclusive products
throughout the catalog, you encourage the customer
to look to you for these special products. Exclusivity
brings credibility to your catalog company in a way
with which other catalogs cannot compete.

55. Arranging Exclusive Listings for Products: The Pluses and Minuses of Seven Different Methods

To get an exclusive product listing in your catalog,
you need to be familiar with the types of exclusive ar-
rangements which are available. Consider these seven.

1. Open-end mail order exclusive gives you the
sole authority to sell a product by mail, through cata-

logs, newspapers, magazines, or television. However, retail stores may also sell the product.

Plus: Mail order sales are unlimited and depend on product desirability and your marketing ability. No other company may sell the product by mail; competition is not a worry.

Minus: Your sales volume may not be large enough to allow the manufacturer volume production; therefore, product cost may be high. Your retail price may not be viable. Competitors may knock-off the product (make a similar product, often for less money) and capture a greater share of the sales. Retailers may use the product for a loss leader, cutting the retail price below what you can offer. If the market becomes saturated, sales will diminish.

2. Catalog exclusive gives you permission to sell through catalogs only. The manufacturer may sell to other media and other types of mail order, or may give permission to another company to do so. Retail stores may also sell the product.

Plus: Good, repeat mail-order buyers will purchase from you. Proper outside list rental can spur product sales, as well as increase the number of quality names for your house list.

Minus: Higher product cost because of lower volume usage. The manufacturer may lose interest because of low sales volume and a binding low profit agreement. Possible knock-off situation.

3. Distributor exclusive. The manufacturer gives you total sales responsibility: mail order, wholesale, retail.

Plus: You have control of the product. You can dictate where it will be sold and influence retail pricing. You need not sell to competitors.

Minus: Operation may become unwieldy. Can you deal with a sales staff who sells wholesale to retail stores? Do you have internal systems to handle wholesale and retail orders? Can you still handle your prime business, mail order? Many companies are not this elastic.

4. Guaranteed sales exclusive gives you the sole right to sell a product by mail as long as you meet a specified sales volume within a stated time period.

Plus: You know how many units you must sell and can plan your advertising accordingly. There's no competition.

Minus: If the sales requirement is not met, you lose the exclusive and could be charged additionally for each unit because of low volume usage. Competitors could knock-off the product, selling at a lesser price and grabbing a large share of the market. If the product is a bummer, you are stuck with a quantity to dispose of, often at a loss.

5. Time-limit exclusive gives you the sole right to sell a product by mail for a specific period of time. It can be six months, one year, or more, depending upon your agreement.

Plus: You have the product to sell during its initial, prime selling period (generally six months to a year). No competition. If the time period is short, knock-off fear is minimal.

Minus: The product may prove to be a poor mail-order seller. A dollar penalty may be assessed if sales volume is not met or time period is not completed. Costs could be high because of low-volume usage.

6. Space exclusive gives you the sole right to advertise and sell the product through magazines and newspapers.

Plus: The consumer must buy from you to get the product. A good product will bring in high dollar volume, plus new names for your catalog.

Minus: The product may fail. You could be obligated to sell a large quantity of units or run a specific amount of advertising, regardless of response. Knock-off possibilities are high.

7. General mail-order exclusive is the right to sell the product through the mail. Other mail-order companies may sell it too. Not sold retail.

Plus: The product is not available to the consumer anywhere else, other than by mail, so sales should be good. Retail store price-cutting is not a worry.

Minus: Other mail order companies can offer the item. Product sales may soon suffer from "mail-order fatigue," too many catalogs carrying the product. Open competition may encourage price cutting and cheap knock-offs.

General Hints:

1. *Try to test a product before agreeing to an exclusive.*

2. *Be financially prepared to back a product with needed advertising or catalog space—you may find another Pet Rock!*

3. *If you are the only company running a successful product which has wide appeal, the product will not go unnoticed . . . competitors will knock it off within a very short time and rob you of sales. Be prepared. (Sadly, most patents offer thin protection.)*

4. *Exclusives provide an opportunity for good sales copy telling the customer it's your very own. Many catalogers use this approach successfully.*

As you can see, a sales exclusive—no matter what kind—can be both good and bad. The decision to look for exclusives is yours!

☐

56. A Celebrity Endorsement Brings Instant Fame to Your Catalog or Product

Customers with special interests in areas such as food, cosmetics, glamour or sports usually recognize prominent people in those fields. This recognition factor creates a wonderful merchandising opportunity of which few catalogers take advantage—that of celebrity endorsement. This method of advertising furnishes the advantages of two major merchandising techniques: the *Attention Grabber* and the *Authority and Credibility Builder*.

Two catalogs that have utilized this approach for many years are Omaha Steaks and Eva Gabor Wigs by Paula. Both promote celebrities in media ads and catalogs. The simplicity of approach used by Wigs by Paula in its media ad shown in Figure 37 is very effective. Because the celebrity is so well known, all that is needed to draw the viewer's eye is a glamorous photo of Eva Gabor. Combine that with the headline "Free Catalog" and the catalog request is garnered. The word "WIGS" displayed prominently in two places

Figure 37

functions as an interest-qualifier. When the customer receives the catalog, the large picture of Ms. Gabor on the cover is seen immediately. Quick association is made ("That's the catalog I sent for!"), eliminating any chance that the catalog could be discarded by mistake.

Omaha Steaks (Figure 38) relies more heavily on the product being sold than on the celebrity to grab the customer's attention. But this catalog house is selling a product in the ad, not merely soliciting a catalog request. Its celebrity, gourmet chef James Beard, was used to feature a cookbook "free with your order," thereby lending credibility to the quality of the steaks and spiriting the customer to order.

Each company has used a celebrity to grab attention in its ad. Wigs by Paula uses the technique as the main area of focus, and Omaha Steaks uses it secondarily. Wigs by Paula concentrates on the lure of a recognizable famous person; Omaha Steaks concentrates on using the name "James Beard" (which was

actually more recognizable than his photo) as an authority/credibility selling point. In the Omaha Steaks catalog, Beard's name is merely mentioned on the order form flap, promoting his exclusive recipes to complement the steaks. The reliance for sales is on the quality of the product line, with the celebrity used to lend authority. Because wigs are a more commonplace product and they need glamorizing for ultimate appeal, Wigs by Paula follows through more strongly with the use of the celebrity.

Today's catalogs are veering more and more into specialized areas, allowing greater opportunities to use celebrity endorsements. Perhaps this is just the technique to enhance sales in your book!

□

Figure 38

57. Merchandise Your Credibility: Four Ways to Increase Sales

Never before has it been so important to establish and build credibility. The rapid rate of new company start-ups has made competition fierce, and the battle for the consumer catalog dollar is on. One way to get your fair share is to establish your credibility so customers feel confident in placing orders. These four elements will help you build credibility.

1. Company history. What year was your business started? Your *business*, not your catalog's first publication. If you published your catalog two years ago, but you have been in business for twenty-five years, tell your customer about your twenty-five-year-old business. Even if you've started a new division of your company, it still is perfectly valid to say "in business

since 1964" or "serving the public for twenty-five years." Letting the consumer know that you are an established company is one of the best ways to merchandise your credibility.

2. Personal letter. Use a "letter" format to introduce your customer to your company and/or the individuals who run it. (Print the letter inside your front cover, on a wraparound, or on your order form.) The owner, founder, president or some other individual in your company can sign this letter, which adds to its effectiveness. What should the "letter" convey?

- age and history of the company
- your method of selecting and/or manufacturing your products (include systems and areas that are special or unique to your product line or business)
- the benefits of shopping with your company (fast service, individual care)
- the benefits of your strong guarantee

The tone of your letter should fit the tone of your catalog, product line, and the tone expected by the customer to whom you are trying to appeal. If you have a difficult product to sell by mail, such as shoes or wigs, take time in your letter to reassure the customer about product fit.

3. Guarantee. Make your guarantee as strong as possible. Almost without exception you can make your guarantee unconditional (a 100 percent guarantee to return the customer's money if she is not satisfied). Don't be afraid that every product you sell will come back. The fact is that a strong guarantee coupled with fast service encourages a minimal return rate. Naturally this assumes that your product is of average-to-good quality, and not a consumer rip-off.

4. Testimonials. They come from your own customers in your daily mail or through phone conversations. Nothing is more believable or reassuring to a prospective customer than knowing that prior customers have been satisfied with your products and service. Testimonials skillfully placed throughout your catalog and/or order form are strong ways to merchandise your credibility.

Points to Review:

1. Company history. Are you taking advantage of how many years your catalog or company has been in business? Are you ignoring this built-in credibility factor?

2. Personal letter. Are you communicating with the consumer in a meaningful manner, or are you just generalizing with empty words? Worse yet, are you ignoring completely this fine area of credibility merchandising?

3. Guarantee. Are you offering the strongest one possible, or are you letting fear of high refunds water it down with too many qualifiers? Qualifiers that can hurt would be time limits for returning merchandise, demands that merchandise be returned, issuance of credit for future orders rather than refunding cash.

4. Testimonials. Are you utilizing favorable customer comments, or are you throwing this golden opportunity to merchandise your credibility into the wastebasket?

If you are not taking advantage of at least two of these four elements of credibility merchandising, you are losing sales. Make it a point to see how you can use all four in your next catalog.

□

58. The "Letter from the President": How Important Is It?

It's possible, if you're Sears or American Express, that you may not need a letter in your catalog. Even that is dubious, because the letter from the president or one of the staff is vital to cover selling points in a way that is acceptable to the public without sounding like "hype." There are many approaches these letters can take, but they all have a common denominator: the warmth of a "real" person relating on a personal level to the customer. This basic sales tool is important no matter how big a company is. Let's examine parts of letters from three totally different catalogs and see the "styles" they take, and what they do.

Figure 39. Family-style Soft Sell. Cotton Dreams is a great little digest-sized book from a family business that sells only cotton clothing. The child models in the catalog are actually the children of the owners, and each season you see them grow. Here's their "hand-printed" letter from the inside front cover.

Figure 39

Dear Friend,

We always love putting together our spring catalogs and working with the new soft and light fabrics and colors, reflecting the warmth and freshness of the season. Two things remain constant—our complete effort and concern for the families we serve, and the quality of the products we represent.

We believe it is the responsibility of Cotton Dreams to provide you with the best selection, quality and values for your family's natural fiber clothing needs.

Please continue to write. We love hearing from you . . . .

Warm regards,

Cheri, Rick Jamin, Shana & Teren Nichols

What a great little note! Pick up those buzzwords? New, Soft, Light, Warmth, Freshness, Families, Serve, Quality, Responsibility, Love. The sincere, good feelings this note engenders probably could enable the sale of used cars in that catalog!

Figure 40. Hard Sell and Savings. Prism Optical is an excellently run company that competes against chain drug stores to sell prescription eyeglasses by mail. No easy task. It's a hard-sell situation, and this letter shows how to "hit 'em between the eyes!" Quality, Durability, Fashion, Savings, Years of experience, Hundreds of thousands sold, Nobody does it better, Repeat customers (we must be good!), Endorsements right in the letter! Relax, it's OK to order prescription eyeglasses by mail from us.

Figure 41. Company/Customer Identification. Mail-order vitamin catalogs are highly competitive. Buyers examine the contents of each pill with the care of a collector assessing his next antique Rolls Royce.

Figure 40

Dear Eyeglass Wearer,

Now *you* can enjoy quality, durability and *fashion* in eyeglasses and save 40, 50, even 60% off regular retail costs! Sounds great, doesn't it?

Over the past twenty-four years we've sold hundreds of thousands of prescription eyeglasses to people just like you. And at this point we have to say that there is no one bigger or better at it than we are—which means *you'll* benefit from *our* experience . . . .

This past year our repeat customers have asked us for more attention to fashion. It seems that looking "just right" is more important than ever. Our standards have always sided towards quality, durability and comfort. To that we now add great looks . . . .

"The glasses are just as good, in my opinion, as what I have paid nearly double for." ". . . every bit as good as you said they would be. Fit fine and looked good . . . ."

Now it's time to sit back and order . . . .

Dear Friend,

I'd like to take this opportunity to introduce myself. I'm Marie Davis . . . your personal shopping representative. No, I'm not the president or the accountant. My job is to make sure that every product in this catalog is the highest quality available—you see, I know what health means to you because it means the same to me, my children, my husband, my parents. I take the same interest in you as I do for me and mine, because we use the products that are offered here ourselves. That's why we can offer you our FIVE POINT GUARANTEE of satisfaction . . . .

Figure 41

Imagine the impression of this letter from Nutrients Best catalog: This company hires someone to do nothing but make sure we, the customers, are getting the best. She even gives this stuff to her kids and her parents! Did you ever see a better, more subtle way of selling based on quality control? Marie Davis' picture appears next to this letter. She is attractive, mid-thirties and pleasant—but stern-faced. Nothing's going to get past this lady! Want to build customer confidence? Here's a company that's got its own ombudsman!

Conclusion: Look at your market position. What makes your company or what you sell special? Now use your letter to tell the folks out there why they should buy from *you?* It's much more believable than a straightforward statement. A "personal letter" lets people know there are human beings behind those pages; it gives them something to relate to that's emotional, not commercial. Make no mistake: when making a choice based on intellect or emotion, people go with their emotions. Use the letter to let them know they're dealing with other people in a friendly, believable atmosphere.

Arthur Pryor, President, Pryorities Advertising, Inc.

59. Don't Overlook Ordering Incentives to Nudge Your Customer into a Purchase

There are seven schools of thought (at least) on ordering incentives:

1. The proponents of never giving away anything: they believe that the best customer is one who doesn't expect something for nothing.

2. Those who believe that free gifts or sweepstakes will encourage more customers, and more dollars in the long run.

3. Those who won't use free incentives to make a sale, but who believe it's extremely worthwhile to induce larger orders.

4. A combination of category 2 and category 3: an incentive is given to make the sale, and further incentives to increase the total dollar order.

5. Those who include free samples with the mailing, hoping that the quality of the merchandise will create the sale.

6. Users of free samples as a "hook," e.g., "first volume free . . . yours to keep whether or not you keep the entire anthology."

7. Promoters of discounts or dollars-off coupons to solicit a sale.

Catalogers who would never involve themselves in free incentives feel that, once started, an incentive program can never (or not easily) be dropped. They find the thought unpalatable that they could be trapping themselves into a possibly-only-mildly-successful program. A strong feeling exists that buyers who need those kinds of inducements do not remain good long-term customers. There is an inclination to believe that, because of this, the main customer list is weak; in other words, a buyer does not a customer make.

High-ticket catalogs don't usually participate in incentives simply because they feel that there is no need to induce a monied customer to spend it, and they don't want to tarnish the class of their image. They often think "why give something away, when the sale will be made anyway?" In addition, it is difficult for a high-ticket catalog to choose as an incentive something which falls into the price expectations of the customer, since most free gifts have to be "cheap." Some feel that an incentive subliminally says "our merchandise isn't good enough to be purchased for itself."

Following are some examples of category 2 incentives, from which you can judge the relative importance placed on the techniques by each cataloger.

Figure 42 shows an incentive presentation by CosmoPedics. The wrap-around cover/order form copy sends you to page 24 for details, where a half page is devoted to the benefits of owning this clock. A pre-printed line on the order form mentions that this gift, which is free with any purchase, requires $2.00 included for shipping and handling, but by this time the customer has already succumbed to the "free with any purchase" gambit and has selected merchandise.

The Gift House has the most subtle free gift incentive we've ever seen. It's not shown on the front or back covers, but is mentioned in the fine print in the "greeting" on page 2. On the inside flap of the order form, there's another copy reference (Figure 43) to the free gift. No area is pre-printed on the order form, because there are no extra charges, and because the

gift is tucked into every outgoing package automatically. It's almost difficult to think of this one as an incentive, since the customer almost has to have already decided on making a purchase before discovering the fringe benefit of the gift.

Beautiful Beginnings (Figure 44) is giving away everything! This presentation is a full page of the order form flap, and is also promoted on the cover. This catalog has a computer-printed wrap-around which mentions the customer by name and also promotes a sweepstakes. Beautiful Beginnings uses plenty of hard-sell incentive techniques. Quite a lot of space which could otherwise have been used to sell actual merchandise has been used for free gifts and sweepstakes, indicating strong belief in incentives.

The wrap-around cover from Hill Brothers (Figure 45) requires the customer to send in a coupon

Figure 43

Figure 44

Figure 42

Figure 45

Figure 46

to receive a mystery free gift. Most of the cover space is devoted to a sweepstakes notice, plus a discount offer of $4.00 off the customer's order. The free gift is a "tag-on."

Figure 46 is an interesting twist on the incentive idea, though it falls in no regular category. This incentive, promoted on the order form, requires an expenditure of $15 from the customer to make her a member of "The Horchow Register." Then, for orders over $100, there's no shipping and handling charge (this alone recoups the membership fee). Gift packages are free instead of costing $1.25 extra. A 15 percent discount is available for L'envoi, Horchow's own cologne. Taken together, it's a very subtle incentive to shop Horchow instead of a competitor.

☐

60. The Negative and Positive Aspects of Catalog Sweepstakes Promotions

A common myth is that customers obtained from sweepstakes do not become repeat purchasers. Not so. They *do* purchase from additional catalog mailings, but the percentage of sweepstakes-obtained customers who become repeat buyers is lower than that of repeat buyers obtained from non-sweepstakes promotions.

So, whenever a cataloger plans to launch a sweepstakes, he should cautiously test the sweepstakes version of the catalog by mailing a non-sweepstakes version to a different segment of the prospect lists.

If you use a sweepstakes, you probably will discover that it will increase your pull by at least three to four times the total number of purchases produced without a sweepstakes. But you may not necessarily produce long-term customer loyalty. You must test and analyze your back-end.

While a sweepstakes will increase the number of orders you receive, it also may reduce the size of the average order, because many of the extra sales are from those who are interested only in the sweepstakes and its prizes.

Many mailers who employ sweepstakes promotions forget that they can mail a second, third or even tenth time to the "no" respondents. A different offer to "no" respondents frequently pulls sufficiently high response to be cost effective. And remember, "no" respondents to a sweepstakes offer can be rented to other marketers just as any direct mail respondent is rented. This is a frequently overlooked income source. The "no" names cannot be merged with the "yes" entries, and they are not worth the same rental price—but rental income from "no" respondents often offsets other costs.

Don't use a sweepstakes with your current customer list. Test it first in acquiring new customers. If it boosts your average order level, as well as your new customer generation, then expand to your customer base. Don't use a sweepstakes unless you're prepared to invest a lot of executive time in thinking it through; analyzing and projecting a campaign; becoming an instant expert; and getting outside expert guidance. Recognize that creative and art costs for sweepstakes are greater than for most other promotions.

One more no-no: don't use syndicated sweepstakes that have not been used successfully by other catalogers. Let someone else waste money testing it. Syndicated sweeps have only a narrow chance for success. Their deadlines are too long. The prizes often aren't appropriate for your audience. And the syndicator gets your names!

René Gnam, President,
René Gnam Consultation Corporation

☐

OFFICIAL RULES

1. Complete the official entry blank and check the appropriate box, then mail this Official Entry/Order Card. Or print "HBO Sweepstakes," your name and address on a 3"x5" card and mail.

2. Winners will be selected in random drawings from among all entries received under the supervision of VENTURA ASSOCIATES, INC., an independent judging organization, whose decisions are final. This offer made by Home Box Office, Inc. Various creative presentations of this Sweepstakes may be used. Chances to win will be determined by the number of entries received. One major prize to a family. No substitutions for prizes offered, with the exception of the Grand Prize where, at the sole discretion of the sweepstakes sponsor, the cash award may be substituted. Trip prize must be taken within one year of notification and is subject to availability. Tax liability is solely that of the winner. The following is the approximate retail value of the prizes: Grand Prize = $7,500, First Prize = $3,000, Second Prize = $250, Third Prize = $120, Fourth Prize = $24.00, Fifth Prize = $14.00.

3. All entries must be received by December 31, 1981. Sweepstakes open to residents of the United States except employees and families of Home Box Office, VENTURA ASSOCIATES, INC., and their various affiliates and agencies. It is not necessary to be a Cable or HBO subscriber to win. All federal, state and local regulations apply. Void where prohibited by law. Winners will be notified by mail.

4. For a list of major prize winners, send a separate self-addressed, stamped envelope to Home Box Office Winners, VENTURA ASSOCIATES, INC.,200 Madison Avenue, New York, NY 10016. DO NOT SEND ENTRIES OR OTHER CORRESPONDENCE TO THIS ADDRESS.

Figure 47

61. Don't Let the Legal Jargon of Sweepstakes Stop You!

Sweepstakes and prize promotions are used effectively by myriad direct mailers to heighten response. Everyone's in the act, from those selling products, subscriptions and services to contribution solicitors. The range of users includes American Express, Sturdee Vitamins, Franklin Mint, Catholic Digest and Spiegels. In short, it appears that effective sweepstakes transcend demographics, concentrating instead on the psychographics of respondents.

Let's look at the basic legal ramifications of sweepstakes. Every state (as well as the Federal government) prohibits "lotteries." A lottery has three elements: prize, chance, and consideration. To legalize a prize offer, any one element must be removed. This is why sweepstakes rules usually state "no purchase required." In this manner, the element of consideration is removed. If one were to eliminate chance, a premium offer would exist, e.g., "everyone who buys and enters gets a key-chain." This eliminates chance, but it also has less power than "you may have already won $25,000!"

Certain states specify other restrictions. North Carolina requires the listing of prize retail values in the rules. New York insists you advise entrants where to write for a list of winners. Florida and New York require that you post a surety bond for the value of the prizes. Legalities discourage some mailers from using the technique. But it's easy to comply with the laws. Independent judging organizations and some lawyers can guide you through the legal maze.

Other regulations refer to claims. Every statement must be documentable and supportable. The "benign puffery" of advertising does not extend to prize promotions. Statements such as "you may have already won," "last chance," "winners guaranteed" must be accurate. Even "lucky number" must mean something is "special" or "lucky" about the number. For example, direct marketers are fond of using official-looking numbers which may, in fact, have nothing to do with the way winners are selected. In such cases, the number shouldn't be referred to as "lucky."

The official rules governing the offer must spell out the terms and conditions of the prize offer clearly and in detail. The rules (a typical set is in Figure 47) must describe the specific method of selecting winners. They are, in fact, the contract between the sweepstakes operator and the consumer.

One last word. Many excellent lawyers who are not experienced in lottery law (and those of us who had a smattering of Business Law 401) often are confused by the definition of "consideration." For lottery law purposes, under Federal regulations consideration is a requirement to buy something in order to enter. Generally, the affixing of a stamp, visiting a store, completing an entry form is not consideration for lottery law purposes. Though the practical application of the lottery law as administered by the U.S. Postal Service is increasingly lenient, many individual states are adding various restrictions. Be sure to contact an experienced judging organization or an attorney experienced in lottery law before proceeding too far down the sweepstakes road.

Ed Burnett, President,
Ed Burnett Consultants, Inc.

62. Combating the Return Factor while Encouraging the Customer to Order: A Tough Job for the Merchandiser

The returned-goods factor must be kept to a minimum in the repeat mail-order business. Steps must be taken *prior* to the customer's decision to order. But what can be done to keep the return factor low without discouraging order placement? The solution is to gear your catalog toward explaining and describing your merchandise so that what the customer receives meets his expectations. The problem is to do this in such a way as to not discourage the placement of the order.

Let's look at a category where complaints and returns run high and where the consumer naturally hesitates to place an order for fear of dissatisfaction— the apparel business.

An apparel catalog which meets the challenge of keeping a low return factor while encouraging an order is Lands' End. Throughout the catalog, it has done an exceptional job of explaining what materials are used, what features make its products superior—and it has supported this with illustrative diagrams. The most important feature is a measurement and conversion chart which occupies two-thirds of the back of the order form (Figure 48). At the top of the chart, the customer is reassured by being told that Lands' End clothing is traditional in size. The illustration shows how to measure for various types of clothing; a conversion chart eases the customer's mind even more. All these features act as insurance against returned goods.

The chart's simplicity makes it easy to interpret; a conversion table telling what size to order for each article makes it even simpler. The problem of size, which once was complex and produced a high return

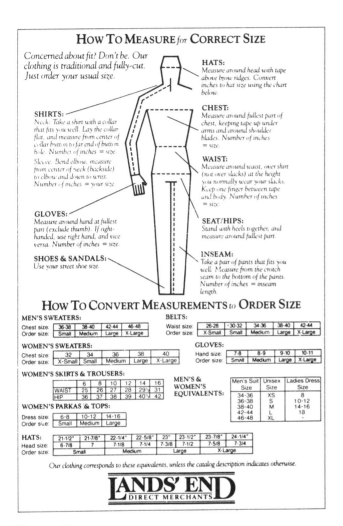

Figure 48

factor, now is solved! Now ordering becomes almost automatic.

The chart is not new or revolutionary, but it accomplishes two things. First, it puts the customer's mind at ease about what size to order, thereby encouraging the placement of an order. Second, it assures more accurate ordering, thereby decreasing the percentage of returns due to improper size. It's a good example of what a merchandiser can do to lower returns before order placement without discouraging an order.

□

63. Satisfaction Guaranteed! Words to Live by if You Want Repeat Mail-Order Business

What does a guarantee mean to the customer? Good products. Good service. Dependability. Credibility. It means he can order in confidence and get his money back if not satisfied. Some would contend that a customer who has had a problem handled quickly and to her complete satisfaction can be an even more loyal continued customer than one who has simply enjoyed an uneventful transaction. The guarantee is the all-important qualifier.

The merchandiser determines the tone and strength of the guarantee. The following six are basic to most guarantees and can be used as guides in establishing or modifying your existing guarantee.

1. Limited time period. Dissatisfaction must be expressed within a specifically stated time period, such as 7, 12, or 30 days. Users: mostly newer, medium to high-ticket catalogers.

2. Unlimited time period. No time period is stated for the customer to express dissatisfaction. The

customer's money must be returned whenever requested, two weeks or five years after purchase. *Users:* older, established catalogers, high and low end; a *few* newer catalogers.

3. Delayed payment. A "free" examination period allows the customer to determine satisfaction before making payment or returning the goods. The examination period is usually no more than ten days. Users: book offers; direct mail pieces for single products; business/industrial catalogers.

4. Replacement. Return merchandise for exchange or credit toward another purchase (no cash refund), usually within thirty days. Users: general merchandise, gift and clothing catalogers.

5. Time extension. Refund is allowed beyond the normally-stated time period. For example, hunting equipment sold before season extends the regular 30-day guarantee to 90 or 180 days, letting customers test the equipment in season. Users: sporting equipment and garden catalogs.

6. Unexpired. Anytime during a subscription period, the customer may decide not to continue and receives money back for the remaining period. Users: magazine marketers; continuity programs.

All of these guarantees should be unconditional. Whatever the reason for dissatisfaction—product, service, packaging, delivery, or no reason—payment should be returned, if requested. Many companies add conditions to their "unconditional" guarantees, refusing refunds or returns on personalized, laundered, worn, used, or altered items, or for non-delivery to any incorrect address provided by the customer. Some require the merchandise to be returned before exchanging or refunding goods. Decide upon the strongest guarantee you can. It is a persuasive element, assuring customers that they are safe in placing orders.

64. How to Price Shipping Charges

Pricing strategy for catalog shipping charges involves several factors in addition to those of recovery of merchandise shipping costs. Four that you should consider carefully are business positioning, marketing planning, distribution patterns, and drop-shipment patterns.

An upscale business positioning with relatively high item prices either dictates an absorption of average shipping costs into the listed item price, or an individual shipping charge posted next to the item price. The rationale for the posting of individual shipping charges rather than the use of a charge schedule based on number of items or total order size could be the belief that posting of individual charges enhances consumer perception of the value of the item—or conversely, that an interval schedule of shipping charges based on order size or number of items degrades the consumer perception of the value of merchandise items.

Marketing planning considerations are often built into the pricing strategy for shipping charges in order to encourage order size enlargement. All shipping charges may be forgiven if the overall order size exceeds a stated amount, or they may be decreased proportionally as the size of the order increases. You might also consider forgiveness or reduction of charges on prospect promotions and multiple gift orders on customer base promotions.

Shipping charge structuring is often based on geographical zoning in place of, or in addition to, order size intervals. Geographic zoning charges can be inflated or reduced beyond the charges dictated by the economies of distance, in an effort to either encourage orders from favorable distribution areas or discourage orders from unfavorable areas. Shipping charge strategy for a vendor with significant drop-shipment distribution will probably differentiate between the charges for drop-shipped and vendor-shipped merchandise.

The following table shows a variety of shipping charge strategies and how they reflect the characteristics of a number of ready-to-wear catalog vendors:

Name of vendor	Characteristics	Shipping charge pricing strategy
The Talbots	Upscale Classic wear High price	Low flat price for postage ($3.00) regardless of order size
Lilly Pulitzer	Upscale Casual wear Medium price	Base charge for first item ($2.75) with reduced additional charge for other items ($.50)
Honeybee	Mid-scale Fashion-oriented High price	Individual itemized prices
Old Pueblo Traders	Mid-scale Fashion-oriented Low price	Price based on number of items
Lane Bryant	Low-/mid-scale Specialty sizes Low price	Shipping schedule based on weight of order and destination

Arnold Fishman, President, Marketing Logistics

65. How to Establish and Register Your Trademark

Once your company has decided upon the suitable word to distinguish your product or service—and don't forget, that word has to be an adjective if you wish to register it as a trademark—it's time to find out whether or not you can have exclusive rights to it. Determine if any other business has prior rights to this adjective. One way is to retain a company to review the U.S. Patent and Trademark Office records as well as state trademark registration files, and in some cases, trade directories. This company will supply a written report of similar pending or registered names, usually within a few weeks. Similarity in appearance, meaning and sound are areas you'll want to consider after the search material has been received, as well as the dates the terms were first used and the products or services with which they were associated. The final determination is made by the trademark examiner in the U.S. Trademark Office, once you've formally applied for registration.

The key in the businessperson's mind is whether or not an average purchaser is likely to be confused in identifying the proposed trademark with related items using a similar name. These other items do not necessarily have to be in active competition with the aspiring trademark registrant. If the existing trademark holder sells in a similar market, the examiner may deny the new application. For example, if a sporting goods manufacturer has a trademark on a particular baseball, it's feasible that a similar-sounding trademark on sportswear might be denied.

The Registration

After the search and the examiner's approval, the name should be registered with the U.S. Patent and Trademark Office. But the name must be used before it is eligible for a registration application, and it must be utilized in interstate as well as intrastate commerce, if federal registraton is desired. Written application must be made, requiring an identification of the applicant owner, the word, the date it was first used, and a description of the use as well as five specimens of the label, tag or other tangible use of the name. The registration fee is $175, with attorney's fees varying from $400 up.

Now the businessperson has exclusive right to her registered mark anywhere in the country and infringers are subject to civil action. Such actions could recover for the registrant any profits made by the violator, any damages sustained by the owner, and her costs of bringing the action. This includes foreign goods bearing similar marks, which may be turned back at customs.

Erwin J. Keup, Attorney, Law Office Erwin J. Keup

CHAPTER FIVE

Producing and Mailing Your Catalog

PRODUCTION AND MAILING ARE THE NUTS AND BOLTS of the catalog business.

Many good suggestions will come from the suppliers you work with; the following chapter will help you come up with ideas of your own.

☐

66. Where the Money Goes When You're "Buying" Your Catalog

The perennial problem is how to balance what you want against what your budget dictates. Understanding where the money goes will help you determine where you can cut back, and where you can't. These major printing areas affect the price of your catalog:

1. Quantity you order
2. Number of pages
3. Size of each page
4. Choice of paper
5. Number of colors for printing
6. Style of binding
7. Alterations

1. The primary area that determines the price you'll pay for printing your catalog is the quantity you order. This quantity depends on many variables: how many people are receiving the catalog, what type of mailing lists you'll add should the book produce the results you want, whether or not you print amounts for a second mailing (perhaps wrapped with a different cover) at the same time you print the original amount. It's a good idea to have your job quoted in "quantity breaks." Establish a starting point of so many thousands, asking for prices in various increments plus an "additional thousands" cost. You'll see how dramatically the price per catalog will lower as the total quantity goes up.

2. The second area which determines price is the number of pages. Try to stay in signatures (groups of pages printed at one time) of eight or sixteen pages. This enables your book to be printed and folded on press if the quantity is big enough (about 25,000 or more).

3. Then, cost is determined by the size of each page. The standard sizes of 5½″ × 8½″ or 8½″ × 11″ are probably the most efficient sizes in terms of cost. But there are other sizes you can use, like 4¼″ × 11″ or 11″ × 11″. The size you choose is, of course, governed by your desire. But the printer you choose may be able to print one size more economically than another, because this is governed by the sizes of the presses he has available. So, if possible, it's wise to talk this over with the printer you wish to use, or conversely, to get quotes from different printers. These could vary vastly depending on the sizes of their presses.

4. In most "large run" catalogs the item that will cost the most money is the paper. Paper can be bought in various weights and grades, from 32 pound up to perhaps 80 pound, and in color. Most practical for

catalog printing is 50, 60 or 70 pound coated. Offset paper or newsprint can also be used. Part of your decision about which paper to use (in addition to your budget, the quality/mood you wish to create and the type of press on which your job will run) will depend on how your catalog will be used. For example, if the catalog is going to be a long-term shelf item that will be used constantly, perhaps it should have a separate cover of heavier stock.

5. Printing can be done in one, two, three, four or five colors. Most practical are one and four colors, but if your promotion will work better and produce more sales, use two or five colors. Though budget must be considered when choosing how many colors to use, testing sales reaction is the only way to determine if going from a two-color to a four-color job will pay off.

6. How you bind your catalog will also affect the cost. The variations are many: saddle stitching, perfect binding, adhesive binding, spiral binding, collated loose sheets in a binder or folder, or just loose sheets. Discuss binding with the printer from a cost standpoint and also from the usage of the piece. For example, perhaps your book is an office supply catalog. If it is perfect bound, the spine can be printed and it can easily be seen and pulled from a customer's shelf.

7. All of these variables are worthy of consideration when assembling your budget. But there is one item that creates an absolutely unnecessary expenditure: "author's alterations." These are changes you make after your material is supposedly "camera-ready." When customers make changes in the final stage of printing, it adds substantially to the cost of the job. So try to make all alterations before your catalog gets to the printer.

Harvey Kuler, President, Vividize, Inc.

☐

67. How to Use Color and Keep Expenses Down

When it comes to printing, each additional color adds cost. Yet designers need color to assure that certain copy and illustrations stand out. Because of cost, many catalogs end up with black type, adding halftone and line art illustrations with red headline type.

Often forgotten is the effect achieved by combining colors, particularly combinations of the screens of two colors. For example, assume a catalog is printed with dark navy type and bright yellow headlines (these headlines would have to be substantial in point size to tolerate the yellow color). A whole range of green tints can be created by combining screen tints of the blue and yellow.

Percentages of Screen Tints

Blue	Yellow	Combined result
50	20	Aqua
50	90	Lime green
Solid (100)	Solid (100)	Forest green

Other colors can be combined creatively to produce many different shades. Most printers can provide a chart showing the effect of combining various percentages of the process colors. A perusal will show you that 50% cyan and 90% magenta produces an attractive purple, while 70% cyan, 70% magenta and 80% yellow make a chocolate brown. Magenta can be combined with tints of yellow to make many pinks or deep reds.

Four-color catalogs often leave some products as black halftones because of the high cost of color separations. *Duotones* and *tritones* can enhance these illustrations, though thought must be given to the colors chosen. Simple combinations of magenta (process red) and black or yellow and black generally are not very attractive. But cyan (process blue) does combine nicely with black to make appealing duotone shades. Talk to your printer about the possibilities and ask to see samples of duotones and tritones he has printed.

An important point to remember is that the effect of these color combinations is changed according to the type of paper upon which they are printed. For instance, coated papers get their glossy appearance from clay and other coatings that can add a yellow cast to the sheet. Uncoated papers vary in brightness depending upon the type of pulp and the additives used. Paper tint affects color reproduction even on ivory stocks, though you may feel that these changes are subtle enough to be acceptable for your job.

There are vast differences in inks as well. Process inks are transparent and allow light to reflect off the paper surface. Opaque inks reflect light off the layer of ink film. But because no printing ink is completely transparent or completely opaque, the kind of ink used by your printer can greatly affect your color reproduction.

The best insurance is to get a press proof of your duotones and tritones with the inks your printer will use on the exact paper your catalog will use. By looking at your previously printed samples and explaining exactly what is wanted, designers can find interesting alternatives without experimenting with colors on successive, expensive press proofs.

James M. Doyle, Market Research Manager, Webcraft

68. How Color Separations Are Made

You must understand how color separations are made before you can transform your artwork into a rich color plate that will print as a faithful reproduction.

To the separator's eye, all color is made up of just four basic process colors: magenta (process red), cyan (process blue), process yellow and process black. Combinations of these four produces almost any color imaginable. The photoplatemaker begins by separating the four basic colors from your artwork using one of two methods: indirect separation or electronic color scanning. The indirect method, a complex and time-consuming process, uses a camera to shoot a continuous tone and then a halftone negative. Electronic color scanning is much faster because it uses a laser to separate the colors and automatically produces four halftone negatives ready for stripping. Both methods separate your artwork into the four basic colors; each has its advantages.

Halftone photography converts your print or transparency into the four basic colors, each being a series of dots of different diameters. This is done by photographing the artwork through a grid pattern much like a window screen in your home. Each color is separated at a different angle of the screen to produce a rosette pattern of dots. (See Figure 49.) If the screen angles weren't varied, each dot would print on top of each other, appearing like a black and white halftone.

Undercover removal. Getting a deep rich black can be a problem. As mentioned above, black results from printing the four separate colors on top of each

Figure 49

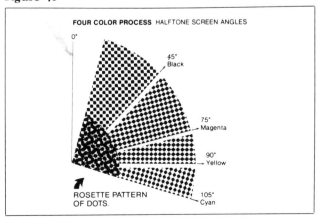

other. But this makes a printed piece appear flat and muddy. Undercolor removal reduces magenta, cyan and yellow and increases black through photographic means or dot etching, thus creating the rich black required for color with definition.

Screen selection. Separators produce the finest quality from your artwork only if they are aware of the paper and inks your printer will use. If the paper is coarse and uncoated, a coarse screen (55 to 65 lines per inch) is required. If the paper is smoother, with a harder finish, a finer screen (150 and upwards) is possible. Your separator should learn the capabilities of your printer's press.

The densitometer enables your printer to more closely match the proof you have supplied. This instrument reads and measures the optical density of your separations and the evenness of the color bars. Color bars are as important as the color proof itself. Without the bars, your printer will be in the dark as to how the film and proofs read across the sheet. If the readings vary during the press run, the color bars help your printer adjust his equipment to match the supplied proof.

Though the densitometer is valuable, it must be used with other available materials. Suppose the printer's densitometer readings are very close to the separator's but they just can't come up to color. The answer is simple, but not obvious. The separator used a warmer red than he should have in order to make the color more vibrant.

Dot etching is the last step taken before your proofs are prepared. The dot etcher goes into the particular area where the size of the dot is off and alters them by hand. They may be thickened or thinned, strengthening or weakening the color perceived in that area. In either case, the dots will be altered so the color matches your artwork.

Contact correction. This technique also thins or fattens the dots. By means of photographic exposure, the dots are reduced or thickened throughout the entire film.

After your separator has shown you proofs and you've approved them, the film is ready to go to the printer for plate making and printing.

Dennis Paul, Production Director, Kobs & Brady

☐

69. Computerized Imaging Systems: How They Can Save You Time and Money

With the introduction of computerized imaging systems, the graphic arts industry has been fully thrust into the space age. But aside from the excitement and mystique of these systems, exactly what do they mean to the catalog marketer?

Before we answer that pivotal question, let's take a quick glance at exactly how these systems work. A computer-based, image-processing system digitizes and displays optical scanner output on a TV monitor. This allows a system operator to perform a variety of functions on artwork ranging from displaying all necessary masks and resizing and replacing art to altering color either locally or overall with digital electronic precision and displaying these changes instantly. These systems enable you to match and create tints, vignettes and windows and finally put everything together with type and display the entire job. It then cuts fully-assembled, one-piece film for printing. Image-processing systems can handle color separations, masking, retouching and dot etching, stripping and proofing.

But enough of the theoretical. Figure 50 shows what computerized imaging did on a job for Cadillac. The client supplied three 2¼″ × 2¼″ transparencies of the three models seen here. They also provided one 3″ × 10″ transparency of the 1986 Cadillac Seville with a model standing in front, plus a mechanical.

Figure 50

The mechanical graphically illustrated how they wanted the final job to appear.

First the transparencies needed retouching. The illustrations were placed in position on the console through a maze of masks, coordinates and edit functions to fit precisely the supplied mechanical. Then the real fun began. Here's what happened, step by step.

1. The color of the existing yellow blouse material was cloned to blank out the back end of the pencil in the model's hand.

2. Wherever two illustrations were placed together—models and the car, model and model—a special blur function was employed so as not to show a hard line. This ensured that the final photograph would not appear to be elements cut and pieced together.

3. A special ghosting function made two models appear as if they are viewed through the car's windows. They seem to have been photographed in this position, not placed there after the fact.

4. The flesh tones of all the models were balanced to give a more real look to the entire piece.

5. A special masking function was used to color balance the grayish background around the three large models, without doing any damage to their hair.

6. On the model at left, an airbrushing procedure created just the right amount of reflection and removed unneccessary glare from her glasses.

7. Cadillac is selling cars, not tennis racquets; the racquet's brand name was removed.

8. The color of the car was enhanced and the chrome was brightened throughout.

A lot of work to be sure. Conventionally, if it were even possible, it would take forever. But with a computerized imaging system, it was manageable, and was done in a relatively small amount of time. What does this mean to you? It means that you can do that which was previously unimaginable in manipulating art and developing layouts for your catalog. It means reduced costs. You can avoid expensive location shooting and reshoots just to drop one new element in a photo. And you can save time and make changes much closer to deadline. So the bottom line is time and money—two things all of us would like to save.

Zane Tankee, President,
Collier Graphic Services

70. Why Do Beautiful Engraver's Proofs Sometimes Print Poorly?

Here's the problem: Different segments, signatures, pages of your press proofs are a big disappointment, even though the engravings you saw were great. This problem can recur constantly unless you take certain precautions.

1. Always proof your engravings on the paper on which your job will run. Too often, engravers will pull proofs on 70# or 80# coated stock, naturally wishing to show their engravings in the best possible light. This is fine if you are going to run your catalog on the same stock. But if you print on paper that is lighter in weight and grade, the engravings you approved will not be reproduced faithfully when you run the job. The paper also could have greater opacity, while yours has more show-through. This is particularly important if your page has large ink coverage.

2. Always check color bars at the top of engraver's proofs. Most engravers will proof your job using a densitometer to check color balance across the sheet. Sometimes, in order to complete a job and please the customer, an engraver will force color into a proof which cannot be reproduced on press. This is done by adding the additional color (be it red, blue, black or yellow) across the sheet in those restricted areas which need the additional single color. The engraver is not doing anyone a favor by showing you proofs that you can sign and approve, but which cannot be duplicated on press.

3. The proper rotation of colors and inks is necessary. When your engraver prepares to proof your job, he must contact your printer to discuss the order in which the colors will run. Is it black, blue, red, yellow . . . or blue, red, yellow, black? Proofing the job in the proper rotation will give you on press what you have seen and approved in the engraver's proofs. Also, you or your engraver must ask what specific inks your printer will use, since this too can affect the printability.

4. Check the quality of retouching on dyes or chromes. Although a dye manufacturer can add additional color to your photograph, you must make sure that these colors can be translated to four-color printing. In some cases, when a dye has deeper hues in the background (dark blue, for instance), it might be necessary to use a fifth color to obtain the color background you have approved in your dye.

Your engravings are only as good as the chromes or dyes supplied. Do not accept something with which you are unhappy, hoping the engraver will improve on it. This does not occur. At best, it's very difficult to transfer to paper the brilliancy you see in a chrome. When viewing chromes, you force light through film; when printing, you are approximating that image. Remember, printing is the approximation of your art—seldom its duplication.

Frank Gesualdi, Production Director, Rapp & Collins

□

---

71. How to Get Proper Bids on Your Printing Job

Getting bids on your printing is an important part of purchasing. Competitive sealed bids are the preferred way to obtain the best price; competitive bidding takes advantage of seasonal soft markets or a printer's down time.

Prepare a bid sheet containing the following points. This is the only way you can be sure that all bids will be based on the same set of specifications.

1. **Title.** This allows you to identify the job so that you and/or your printer will be able to call the job by a common name.

2. **Unit.** Identifies the type of job: folder, booklet, letter, envelope, catalog, etc.

3. **Quantity.** The amount you wish to purchase. It's a good idea to investigate quantity cost breaks as well.

4. **Size.** Is it 8½″ × 11″ or 5½″ × 8½″, or whatever size you choose?

5. **Number of lots.** This identifies multiple versions for testing different copy, using different codes, etc.

6. **Fold to.** Does the letter or brochure fold to fit a #10 envelope, a 6″ × 9″ envelope, or is it a fancy fold?

7. **Number of pages.** The catalog could have 8, 16, 24, 32 or more pages. The letter could be 2, 4, etc., pages.

8. **Colors.** Is it 2, 3, 4 colors? Does it print one or two sides of the sheet?

9. **Bleed.** Does the ink run off the page (without margins) making it bleed? Bleeds usually cost more.

10. **Ink coverage.** Too often a purchaser may forget to establish ink coverage when bidding a job. This is very important when you consider the press sheet could have very light ink coverage (20%) and a great deal of white space, or heavy ink coverage (75 to 85%), which can influence reproduction of the job.

11. **Stock.** Here you must establish the kind of paper (coated, uncoated) you will be using. Always specify the name of the sheet or grade, e.g., number 1, 2, 3 grade. Often a purchasing agent will think she's getting a great buy, only to discover that the printer has substituted an inferior grade of paper to lower the price. A printer recommending an alternate stock should specify its name and grade.

12. **Art and preparation.** Here you must specify how your art will be prepared. For example, if you are supplying four-color mechanicals, will your transparencies be 35mm or 5″ × 7″? If your four-color art is assembled in position, how many assemblies will there be? If your mechanicals are two-color, will the second color be an acetate overlay? Is all color type indicated properly?

13. **Finishing and binding.** Does your catalog have a saddle stitch? Does it perfect-bind or side-wire stitch?

14. **Proofs.** If the printer is doing your color separations, how many blues do you need? Will you accept color keys of some type, or do you want full-color press proofs? How many sets do you need? Do you expect a second press proof, adding to the cost, or are chromalins acceptable? (Chromalins are a less expensive way of seeing color. Using scanners, color separators now can supply excellent chromalins for approval).

15. **Packing.** Should the printed material be delivered bulk, in cartons, on skids? Packing material in cartons is more costly.

16. **Destination.** Will the printer deliver the material to your mailing house or distributor?

17. **Delivery date.** When must all material arrive at its destination?

In addition, ask suppliers to separate costs into four categories: printing, paper, separations, and freight. Some printers have a tendency to low bid a job, knowing they can make up the differences in author's alterations. Asking for a breakdown will force them to be up front with each item. Also, the use of a lesser grade of paper would be highlighted in the individual cost breakdown. This is also true of color separations.

If you follow the outline above, all your printers will bid on the same specifications, and you'll be able to make an apt comparison. You'll also have a much happier association with your printers.

Frank Gesualdi, Production Director, Rapp & Collins

72. How to Determine What Kind of Paper You Want

The material that will show your product is paper and it should be selected with the same care used in choosing your photographer, separator and printer.

Consider features such as finish, grain, weight, and bulk. These areas will affect print quality and price.

Finish refers to the feel and smoothness of the sheet. You can use paper as it comes from the driers of a paper machine, or you can buy machine-calendered paper for a smoother finish or super-calendered paper for an even smoother finish. (Calendered is a term indicating that paper has been smoothed by passing through rollers). For even smoother finishes and paper with better ink holdout, you will have to buy coated paper. (Holdout is ink's ability to sit on the paper rather than being absorbed into it.) Coated papers can reproduce finer halftone screens and have greater ink holdout and higher opacity than uncoated sheets. Application of a coating, from a dull finish to a very glossy finish, can control the weight and bulk of a sheet to give you the look and feel you require for your catalog.

Weight and bulk. With few exceptions, paper is identified by basis weight in pounds of a ream (500 sheets) in its grade size.

Grades of Paper

Book	Bond	Cover	Bristol	Index
25″ × 38″	17″ × 22″	20″ × 26″	22½″ × 28½″	25½″ × 30½″

For example, 500 sheets (1 ream) of 100# book (25″ × 38″) weighs 100 pounds. 500 sheets of 50# cover (20″ × 26″) weighs 50 pounds.

When selecting your stock, keep in mind that, in addition to the weight of the sheet, you will want to know how much that sheet bulks. Bulk for book paper is expressed as the number of pages per inch for a given basis weight. For example, the bulking range for a 50# book stock can vary from 310 to 800 pages per inch.

Grain. When ordering paper, the grain direction should be considered for three reasons: (1) Paper folds smoothly with the grain direction and roughens or cracks when folding across grain; (2) paper is stiffer in the grain direction; and (3) paper expands or contracts more in the cross direction when exposed to

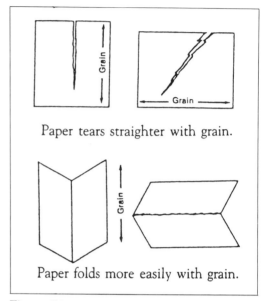

Paper tears straighter with grain.

Paper folds more easily with grain.

Figure 51

moisture changes. In Figure 51 are a few simple tests that will show how paper tears and folds.

Print quality. Paper *color* plays a large role in how your piece will look after it is printed. Type, for instance, is more easily read on a soft white, while process colors are most accurately produced on a neutral white. *Brightness* of paper affects the contrast, brilliance and snap of the printed subject. Artificial brighteners added to paper can affect reproduction because most are not neutral in color, but have excess blue reflectance. *Opacity* refers to the show-through of the printed image from the opposite side of the sheet or the adjoining sheet. Opacity is affected by the thickness of the sheet and the use of fillers like titanium dioxide. *Gloss* affects the appearance of the ink film on the paper. *Refractiveness* relates to the light absorption of the paper's surface or coating. It can cause halftones to appear darker than they should.

When placing orders for large runs, your printer and the mill should work closely to determine the exact specifications for your job. Because web shutdowns cost time and money, rolls must be properly wound, protected, stored on end, and have good tensile strength to minimize tearing or breaking on the web. Your paper should be uniform in thickness, free from scum, holes, spots, slitter dust, fiber picking and lint. Your paper should have a minimum of contraction and expansion, contain a minimum number of splices and have sound cores for winding and delivery.

Dennis Paul, Production Director, Kobs & Brady

☐

73. How to Calculate the Press Run for Your Catalog

The key factor in setting a press run is determining the exact number of names to be mailed. Calculating this quantity before the merge-purge is finished begins with the original mailing list orders. These quantities become more exact as the run counts for each list selection become available after the lists are run by your list maintenance house.

The original mailing list orders get "scrubbed" as the individual tapes arrive at the merge-purge house and are logged in by the tape librarian. After the gross input quantities of each computer tape are determined prior to the merge, the calculation of net output becomes a process of evaluating duplication rates and estimating the net output.

If the final merge-purge results are available enough in advance of your press run, calculating quantity is straightforward. Just total the net quantities for each drop and add any additional catalogs for uses other than mailing. But you need to calculate the press run as far as possible in advance. Sales forecasts need to be maintained, budgets must be planned and the printer needs to order paper as well as calculate time and volume demands on his press.

In addition to setting the press run quantity for the catalog, you need to determine the quantity for the order forms. You need more order forms than catalogs because of bindery spoilage. The question is: How many more? Ask your printer to make a recommenda-

tion, taking into account the size of the press run, the reputation of the order form supplier and the efficiency of the bindery operation. Your printer may require overruns of two percent. But if you do not specify the exact press run, including overs, the order form printer may give you (and charge for) four percent over the original order. You should plainly spell out the quantity of catalogs and order forms you will print and the amount of overrun you will pay for.

Review your press run with your printers. It's useless to work out attractive pricing only to print thousands more catalogs than you need. Unused catalogs are a genuine waste—you cannot even sell coated stock to the paper merchants. Careful planning can save you a considerable amount over the course of a year.

The first step in calculating your print run is to outline the versions of each catalog, the mailing dates and the gross input of names for each version.

Drop 1: September 20   Cover "A"   Quantity, 250M
Drop 2: October 20   Cover "B"   Quantity, 1,200M
Drop 3: November 15   Cover "B"   Quantity, 250M

How do you estimate the gross input of the merge-purge? Develop a "list of lists" which includes each segment of the house file to be mailed and all the rental lists. The "list of lists" should include the following:

List Name   Quantity Received
Key Code   Date Received
List Broker   Amount of Names into Merge
Quantity Expected

The second step is to estimate the net output from the merge-purge. In this example, the gross input of names is 1,700M and includes house names, inquiry names and rental names. The net output is calculated by multiplying the gross input quantity times the average duplication rate. Your own historical duplication rates are the best indication of what your duplication rate will be. It makes sense that if an earlier merge duplicated at 25 percent using a similar mix of house names to rental names, and the same variety or mix of prospecting names, then you should experience a similar duplication rate. In a typical merge-purge the house file and multibuyer files will have priority over the rental lists, so *the majority of duplicates will come out of rental names.*

Next, add up the various list segments, drop dates and versions. In our example, the three drop date quantities total 1,700M. This mailing quantity plus 22M for package inserts and retail store distribution brings the total requirement to 1,722M copies. The sample press run calculation worksheet is shown here.

Calculation of a Catalog Press Run

Drop 1:	September 20, Cover "A"		
	House file	200,000	
	Spring catalog 2X multibuyer	50,000	
	Total Drop 1	250,000	
			250,000
Drop 2:	October 20, Cover "B"		
	Prospects' gross quantity	1,200,000	
	House file	200,000	
	Spring catalog 2X multibuyer	50,000	
	Total gross input	1,450,000	
	Duplication percent = 25% (from rented lists, not house file)		
	Net output from merge-purge	900,000	
	less Drop 1	(250,000)	
	Net output Drop 2	750,000	
			750,000
Drop 3:	November 15, Cover "B"		
	Remail of house file	200,000	
	Package inserts/store use	22,000	
	Net output Drop 3	222,000	
			222,000
Total Press Run			1,222,000
Cover "A"			250,000
Cover "B"			972,000
Order Form press run at 102%			1,246,440

Jim Coogan, Vice President, Woodworker's Supply

☐

74. The Benefits of Ink Jet Printing

Ink jet printing is recognized as the most versatile, cost-effective addressing and personalization method available today, yet many catalog producers are afraid of this useful technology. After learning some new terminology and production procedures, anyone who has coordinated a mailing using computer-generated labels will be able to produce an ink jet mailer. In fact, using ink jet printing can be easy and not costly.

The benefits of ink jet addressing and personalization should convince hesitant catalogers to give this new technology a try. Here are a few benefits:

1. Cheaper. Ink jet requires no paper or glue and can be significantly less expensive than labeling. (But costs vary, and ink jet may not be economical for the catalog with small distribution).

2. No Lost Names. Once a label is destroyed (and many do get stuck together or cut apart) that name is lost. But a name that is destroyed during production of ink jetting can be regenerated by replaying the tape.

3. Faster. Labels are produced on a line printer and affixed by a labeler. Ink jet is a one-step process.

4. Versatile. Personalization data can be added to a piece as it is addressed. For example, ink jet permits display of past customer purchasing information on the outside of the catalog, the most common use of data-base marketing.

Further, ink jet information cannot fall off or be stripped during post office handling. Too many labels are unsightly stick-ons to otherwise carefully-designed catalog covers. Ink jet printing now comes in colors and type fonts designed to look like script or typewriters.

Many binderies offer ink jet printing on their saddle-stitching or perfect-binding equipment. Some are able to provide ink jet on the cover only, while others offer variable data on more than one signature. Ink jet printing is also offered by some suppliers of outerwraps and bind-ins.

When the ink jet system is applied "in line" on web presses, it can provide a large personalization area, offering the cataloger the opportunity to test various prices on the order form, place customer purchasing data on the outerwrap, assign geographical and list codes on the reply envelope, or drop lucky sweepstakes numbers on the reply device. The marketing advantages of ink jet printing during the addressing process are many, and all should be investigated.

James M. Doyle,
Market Research Manager, Webcraft

☐

75. How to Choose a Lettershop

While the choice of a lettershop is not quite akin to selecting a life's mate, it still must not be made lightly. Catalogers face many choices: artists, photographers, printers, etc. Though all candidates may be good and reputable, one may be more appropriate. What then sets the winner apart?

With lettershops, there are two areas to consider: the physical plant that will produce your work, and the more subtle characteristics of the lettershop, such as style, reputation, organization, procedures, ease of communication, location, postal service relations, and so forth.

Where do you start? If you require a lettershop in your own metropolitan area, begin with your local

Yellow Pages. For lettershops out of your immediate area, perhaps near your printer, there are three sources you can try: the Yellow Pages of one or two locales under consideration; the advice of your printer in the area (who's not likely to jeopardize his work by recommending a substandard mailer); and the trade directory of lettershops world-wide: Mail Advertising Service Association International (MASA), Suite 440W, 7315 Wisconsin Avenue, Bethesda, Maryland 20814. It lists members and the categories of services each member provides.

Each lettershop under scrutiny obviously must have the mechanical ability to process your mailing. If you use $9'' \times 12''$ envelopes and a lettershop does not have equipment of that size, it may be out of the picture, unless other attributes are very attractive. The lettershop may be willing to get the necessary equipment to process your work, an arrangement with clear implications and commitments on both sides. It's mentioned only so the possibility is not overlooked.

The lettershop's capabilities are a good starting place. What do your jobs require? What does the lettershop have? Does it have enough of it? Even these questions are not as simple as they seem. How much is enough equipment? A shop with one labeler and one inserting machine may have enough equipment if it runs three shifts a day and is given the time to produce your job. A shop with fifty machines may be unable to handle your job if that equipment is committed to other customers.

First, know what your mailings need, not just physically but with regard to your list segmentation, presort qualification, geographic concentration, stock changes during labeling and inserting and any other details you can think of. Look for a lettershop which can handle not only your mechanical needs, but also other complexities. For example, simple mailings may not need sophisticated controls. But with complex mailings, you may be uncomfortable with anything less.

Ask each lettershop for a list of equipment. If they don't have one or won't provide one, that may put them out of the picture. If you know precisely what equipment your jobs require, you could ask how many of this machine and how many of that machine the lettershop has. But a complete list will give you a better picture of the lettershop's scope of services. When you get an equipment list, be sure to date it if the lettershop didn't. Most lettershops are in a state of expansion and these lists quickly get outdated. If possible, get a list of services as well as equipment, since you're ultimately interested in what they can do with all that hardware.

□

76. How to Avoid Mailers' Most Frequent Mistakes

After months of selecting and photographing merchandise, copywriting, creating layouts, planning printing and choosing lists, your lists and materials arrive at the lettershop. You sigh with relief knowing the worst of your production job is over.

Then comes a phone call from your lettershop: there's a problem with the mailing. Though it's always possible to discover an entirely new difficulty, you'll be a few steps ahead if you understand the most common problems. Here are two which appear with frustrating regularity at the receiving dock of many lettershops.

1. Probably the problem which occurs most frequently is the improperly configured permit imprint or indicia. The easiest way to avoid going astray is to remember that there are three distinct parts to indicia:

- the type of mail which is being sent
- the statement that U.S. postage has been paid
- the city and permit account into which postage has been paid; or the company that "owns" the mailing (provided the company has been given permission to mail using a company permit)

Let's take them one at a time. The first part is usually one of the following: First Class mail, bulk rate, non-profit organization, or bound printed matter.

The second part *must* read "U.S. postage paid." You may add the amount of postage paid, but why would you? Or you may add the weight of a First Class piece. Periods after the "U" and "S" are optional. The copy may appear on one or two lines. But regardless of the class of mail, this copy is mandatory. Finally, you must show where the mailing originated and its permit account number. Or, if you have permission to use a company permit imprint, the name of the company

Figure 52

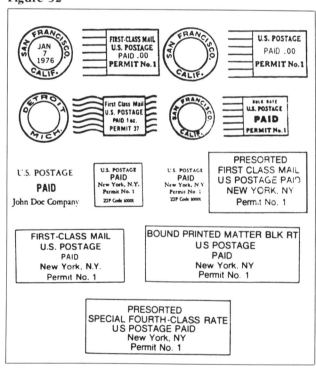

may be substituted for the place of mailing and permit number. Samples of various permit imprints are shown in Figure 52.

For further information on permit mailing, see section 145 of the Domestic Mail Manual (DMM) or contact your lettershop. It's a lettershop's "business" to be thoroughly familiar with all postal regulations and your lettershop can be of enormous help in avoiding errors. But you must contact them and ask your questions before your promotion is chiseled in marble.

2. A second frequent problem is the enclosure that won't fit in the envelope. It is not enough to simply assume that you're safe because your #9 BRE is smaller than a 6″×9″ outer. That's true; but a #9 envelope is 3⅞″×8⅞″ and ⅛″ clearance is not enough for high speed mechanical inserting. You need at least ½″ in length and ¼″ in height. You need more if the enclosed material is bulky. Extra thickness requires extra clearance.

Henry Spitz, Vice President, Brodie Advertising Service

☐

77. How to Mail—and When to Do It

Take these few hints on smoothing out your mailing procedures, and you'll also increase your bottom line.

When you mail, be sure you:

1. Have all lists on labels (cheshire or pressure sensitive) delivered to you, not your fulfillment shop. You and you alone must check labels for quantity, spread, sex, home vs. business address, keys, titles, classification data. Did you get a fifth-digit ZIP select? Were certain states or SCFs omitted? Is there any discernible duplication? Does the list "feel" right?

2. Mail all of a given list in one drop. Staggered mailings will produce staggered returns—which will destroy any half-life examination.

3. Always insist upon a postal receipt verifying the number of pieces placed into the mail stream on a given day. This does two things: it verifies the quantity of mail delivered on a given day, and the Postal Service date stamp gives the actual date mailed.

Sometimes it's better not to mail at all.

1. Do not use direct mail if the order margin is small . . . no matter how great the markup is. For example, a book to sell at $5 with an order margin of $4 (but a markup of several hundred percent) simply will not fly. The minimum cost in the mail is in the range of $225 to $275 per M. At that rate, the cost of promotion requires sales of some 6 percent . . . which just isn't going to happen.

2. Before starting a direct mail program, be sure you ascertain the universe of likely prospects. If this universe, even if doubled by peripheral concepts or classification, is small, it may be best not to mail at all.

3. Do not mail those lists from a merge-purge where the duplication identified indicates little prospect of success.

4. Do not mail secondary segments of a list where the primary or ideal segment has not worked. For example, if current customers of a list have failed, there is no reason to expect older customers from the same list (with the same characteristics) to work. If customers do not work, inquiries unconverted to customer status for the same list surely will not work.

Ed Burnett, President, Ed Burnett Consultants, Inc.

78. Use This Year's Data for Next Year's Decision: When Should You Mail?

When analyzing your customer names, some segments will be identified easily as having outstanding response rate potential. These segments should be used for a second mailing of your Fall/Christmas catalog. This second mailing can be a new book or a "remail" book, a very successful technique for many companies. A remail involves making some not-so-subtle changes to the first book in order to make it look new, without changing merchandise. Use a new cover and a new outside four or eight pages. If these changes are carefully arranged, some of the signatures for the second mailing can be printed with the signatures for the first, reducing printing costs per copy.

Generally, the first Fall/Christmas mailing should be received in the customer's home after Labor Day. Overall response rates suffer when a Christmas-oriented book arrives in a home on August 12th and the temperature is 102 degrees. The second mailing, or remail, should start about October 20th, spreading perhaps over two weeks. Books should not be mailed after November 5th.

The list segments that will receive the second mailing should be sort-separated and mailed first in the first mailing. This provides the maximum time interval between receipt of the two books.

These segments should be established carefully. For example, two-time, three-time and four-time buyers are identified in some company files as multiple buyers, separated by year of last order. Consideration is not given to the time element of last order versus next-to-last order. A current year multiple buyer who last ordered eleven months ago, and whose next-to-last order was three years ago, should not be combined with those who have ordered twice in the last eight months.

There are many successful programs. You must develop yours by experience and detailed analysis. It's the only way to provide an individual answer to "when, and to whom, should you mail."

R. Roy Hedberg, President, Hedberg & Associates

CHAPTER SIX

Marketing Your Catalog to Develop New Customers

MAILING OUT YOUR CATALOG ISN'T ENOUGH. You also need to promote your business through effective advertising.

The following chapter shows how to choose the best possible ways to advertise your catalog.

☐

79. Prospecting for New Customers with a Mini Catalog

Historically, the mini catalog's strongest use is as a promotional tool to acquire new customers. The mini was designed as a ride along and so far has worked most effectively used in this manner. Its success has been due to its low cost to print and distribute. Where traditional methods of prospecting with a catalog for new customers may cost $350 to $600 per thousand, the mini can be printed and distributed for $80 and $100 per thousand.

Where prospecting with a regular catalog might produce ten to twenty customers per thousand with an average order of $60 to $90, a mini catalog may produce 3 to 7 customers per thousand with an average order of $40 to $60. The bottom line is that the mini can provide you with a new customer, not at a cost, but at a profit. An example follows.

Based on reports from marketers who have been prospecting successfully with the mini catalog, customers acquired in this manner will then purchase with the same frequency and average dollar amount as those acquired with a full-sized catalog. And you got those customers in a one-step process! You can mail four to six times more mini catalogs at the same cost you are now paying to prospect with a regular catalog. You can mail to lists you never would have been able to test because of the high risk of solo mail. The mini as a self-mailer has yet to be proven. However, one or two minis have been put in an envelope with a letter and have worked well.

Vernon Carson, Vice President Marketing, Web Specialties

☐

Comparison between Prospecting with a Regular Catalog and a Mini Catalog

Catalog cost (print & mail)	$500/M	Mini catalog cost (print & mail)	$90/M
Customers responding	10/M	Customers responding	5/M
Gross sales	$800/M	Gross sales	$250/M
Margin	50%	Margin	50%
Profit (Loss)	($100/M)	Profit (Loss)	$35/M
Prospecting cost per person	$10	Prospecting cost per person	$0
Profit per customer	$0	Profit per customer	$7

80. How to Create a Mail-Order Buyer

The tendency to mail only to *proven* mail-order buyers creates a mushrooming universe of catalog marketers mailing more and more frequently to essentially the same buyers. But the industry will continue to thrive only if catalog marketers accept the challenge to invest time and money to create new mail-order buyers. Here are a few tips to make the effort pay off.

1. Go after other mail-responsive lists. Direct-mail-sold magazine and newsletter subscribers and direct-mail-generated contributors to various causes are the next best thing to proven mail-order buyers. Many subscriber and donor lists will respond surprisingly well to catalogs.

2. Offer a catalog subscription to magazine subscriber lists. Proven direct-mail-sold magazine subs are good prospects to subscribe to another publication: *your* catalog. Your subscription rate should just cover your costs. Two major mail-order marketers have catalog subscriber lists which convert to new customers just as well as the best performing outside mail-order buyers lists.

3. Support a worthwhile cause. There's no better way to convert mail-responsive donors on fund-raiser lists to mail-order buyers. Consider contributing a percentage of your sales to a relevant cause. One outdoor catalog donates one dollar from each order to the Sierra Club. A high-ticket gift catalog earmarks two percent of sales for various cultural organizations. They heavily promote these efforts in their mailings. The former does well with environmental lists, and the latter with lists of arts and culture supporters.

4. Support your catalog. *Reader's Digest*, Publishers Clearing House, Time-Life and other major mailers support their direct mail with other media.

Broadcast media (both TV and radio) provide excellent support if you've got enough mail going into a particular market. This may require ganging your list selections to provide heavy penetration into a specific market. Additional ways of supporting your catalog are postcard announcements (both before *and* after drops), print advertising and telephone marketing.

5. Make an offer that can't be refused. Why isn't everyone a mail-order buyer? Two basic reasons: inertia and lack of confidence, both of which can be overcome. Produce an inexpensive cover wrap or a bind-in card for catalogs going to outside lists, presenting a special offer for new customers. Offer a discount on an initial purchase, or a credit toward a future purchase. Offer a free gift or special guarantee . . . whatever works to get more nonmail-order buyers to try *your* catalog.

6. Sell a concept in your advertising. More and more catalog marketers are using space ads to generate catalog requests, and are finding that these respondents turn into pretty good mail-order buyers. Lands' End details the well-made quality of its clothes and attracts people who look for top quality *and* a good price—and just may be willing to shop by mail to get it. Royal Silk sells a similar concept, and in that way creates a good number of new mail-order buyers.

Donn Rappaport and Liza Price,
Partners, American List Counsel, Inc.

81. Get a Customer, Not Just a Name!

Mail-order firms have always advertised their catalogs in magazines and Sunday supplements. Small space ads have become a standard advertising method and ambitious publications recently have come up with attractive space rates for catalog sections where your catalog can be displayed with numerous others.

The traditional catalog ad features a small illustration of a catalog cover and a brief description of the kinds of products available inside. Because of the cost of publication space, these ads are usually an eighth of a page or less in size. Sometimes $1 or $2 is requested to qualify a prospective buyer and defray the costs of advertising and mailing. Occasionally a rebate of this fee is offered to respondents who make a purchase.

But does this convoluted advertising process ignore the fundamental of direct response marketing? After all, the primary goal is to attract buyers, not browsers. While some marketers spend advertising dollars to display catalogs in space ads, others get orders directly by promoting carefully selected products. Mail-order companies such as The Sharper Image, Early Winters, Royal Silk and Fingerhut have been successful selling distinctive products, not just catalogs, through Second-Class publications.

New techniques and devices are available to trigger plenty of creative thinking on how to increase response to a space ad. Bindable booklets, mini-catalogs and novelty formats (Figure 53) like pop-ups can be inserted next to those ads. These vehicles are extremely interesting devices which accomplish several of the following direct marketing goals:

1. Attract attention. A bound-in insert is a "bookmark" which brings readers to your ad by causing a natural "break" in the pages. The problem of position is avoided.

SOME MAGAZINE "BOOK MARK" INSERT FORMATS

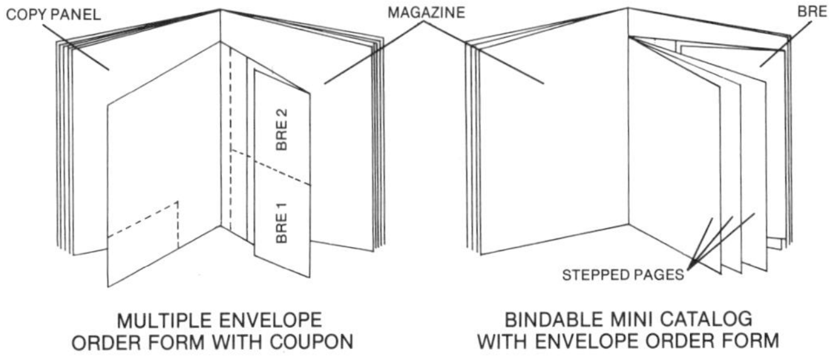

Figure 53

2. Allow easy order placement. A bound-in reply device can be detached easily by prospective buyers. This helps encourage impulse purchases.

3. Get payment up front. A bound-in business reply envelope brings back cash or confidential credit card information. This improves front-end cash flow.

Bound-in reply devices are more expensive than the usual advertising methods, but you may find that their advantages will more than pay their way. Magazine "bookmark" inserts are innovative direct response marketing tools, and as such may warrant your investigation and testing.

This step forward for direct marketers is not without problems. Many publications would rather sell space and will not allow novel inserts. Other publications are unable to find suppliers for these exciting formats. Coordination of an insert intended for more than one publication can be difficult if your printers are not familiar with binding methods, insert specifications and publication procedures. An experienced direct response printing company can help solve these problems, offer cost-saving recommendations and make your promotion worry free.

The benefit of product advertising on "bookmark" inserts is to get a customer, not just a name. Savvy direct marketers can test different products and prices in magazines targeted at specific demographic groups. The challenge is to make mail-order advertising more dynamic and cost effective. Novel "bookmark" formats can help direct marketers meet this challenge.

George Lane, Advertising Manager, Webcraft

☐

82. Don't Be Afraid to Offer Your Catalog in Space Ads

It's surprising how many catalogers are hesitant to run a space ad advertising their catalog. A common concern is "My elegant catalog costs a lot to produce. Its image is upscale and people expect us to look expensive. Wouldn't offering a free catalog in space be counterproductive?"

Here's where the value of testing is apparent. Offering an elegant catalog free should not tarnish your image. Few people who receive something free ever complain about not having to pay, especially if it has value. For your company, it's really a matter of economics. Will you get enough qualified leads with a satisfactory conversion rate to pay for the catalogs you give away?

Many mailers are nervous about offering a free catalog in space but not about sending free catalogs to rented lists. Remember that the space lead has to invest time and a stamp to get your catalog, which makes him a good risk—maybe far better than a rented name. It's important to have qualified leads to keep waste minimal, but ways to qualify inquiries without charging for the catalog can be handled in the ad copy and coupon. The first qualifier is the media you select. Be sure it's on target. As you get into more sophisticated testing you may try different qualifiers in different publications, especially where conversions are accept-

able but the cost of leads is high. In testing a free catalog offer versus charging, start with $1 and work up in dollar increments. Experiment with applying the price of the catalog to the respondent's first purchase.

Carl Bloom, President,
Bloom & Gelb, Inc.

☐

83. How to Decide Which Item to Run in Your Space Ad

Deciding whether to run one item or several in a single space ad is an issue that is controlled greatly by the amount of space you want or can afford to buy. But let's say you've determined the vehicle in which you want to advertise: the magazine with readers you feel will respond to your product line. You merely want to try a small ad, sized to accommodate just one item. What are the criteria for choosing that item?

1. Don't choose an item you've never run before in your catalog. This is not the place for testing new items. Your main reason for advertising in space is to get new customers. The best way to be sure of response is with a tried-and-true item.

2. Choose one of your most popular items. This is a direct outgrowth of the first point. The item that has the best chance of selling is one that you know has sold well before. In addition, the names you are after are those that will fit your catalog's existing customer profile. There's no better way to add names that are likely to respond to your other products, than by getting them to buy an item that properly represents your product line.

3. Choose an item that has a good profit margin. After you narrow your field of selection to your most popular items, consider first the ones with the healthiest profit margins. The logic of this is obvious, but don't forget that shipping weight can be a hidden cost. The lighter the item and the easier it is to pack, the better.

4. Choose an item that is readily available from your supplier source. And to be *sure* of availability, check first with the supplier. Suppose your ad goes "gangbusters?" Suppose it pulls a response that requires twice as many units as you have in house? And what happens if your supplier says, "Sorry, no more available for two months." When you're fortunate enough to get response, you don't want those wonderful new names sitting around waiting forever for fulfillment. A delay like this ensures that your company makes an initial, bad impression; those new customers may never order from you again.

5. Choose an item that you can present effectively in small space. An item that sells well in your catalog but needs an inset line drawing to show various "hidden" points is not the best item to show in a small space ad. Neither is one that needs tons of copy to describe its valuable assets.

6. Choose an item from the lower retail end of your line, rather than the higher end. You are likely to receive more responses to the lower ticket item than to the higher one. If your space ad pulls sales of $3,000, and your item sells for $100, you'll get thirty names. If it sells for $10, you'll get 300 names. Since the object of the ad is to build your mailing list, it makes sense to try to get more names. In addition, it's usually quite difficult to sell high-ticket items in small space ads.

7. Consider including postage with the retail price ("only $9.95 postage paid") in order to save valuable copy space.

8. Consider including acceptance of charge cards as payment method. This offers an easy way for the customer to make the purchase. Charge card names are also good future customers.

The last two suggestions are subsidiary issues to the selection of the item in the first place, but they do indicate the many areas of thought which go into the development of an effective space ad.

☐

84. Small Space Ads: Don't Forget the Headline Is the Grabber

The headline must instantly convey the most essential point about the item shown in your ad. Consider the competition that occurs on a single magazine page crammed with ads. Each ad on one of these pages hopes to get the reader's attention and response; each one tries to fit every possible detail into the ad. The problems of clean design are compounded by all this competition and by information difficult, but necessary, to convey to the reader in a single small space. This information must include not only the copy sizzle and data about the item, but also the basic ordering details.

Each of these elements is really a separate problem—but the one we will dwell on here is the headline. Your first decision about the headline is what to say and how to say it clearly. The second is to choose typography that will show it as clearly as you've said it. If the headline does not immediately transmit the main idea of the item, it is not working hard enough for your advertisement.

Figure 54 and Figure 55 are full-sized reproductions of ads shown in the *House Beautiful* page. Let's compare their impact.

Figure 54

Figure 55

Figure 56

Figure 57

Figure 54 uses a headline of descriptive adjectives but omits the name of the item. Traditional, yet modern *what?* Item prices are printed as prominently as the vague headline, a technique usually reserved for an outstanding price structure. Yet these prices are not unusually reasonable. Though the typeface is clear, uncluttered, and readable, it is somewhat small, especially when compared to the size in which the prices are printed. The ad would have drawn more attention by beginning with "The Finest Brass Candle Stands," adding "Traditional, yet Modern" as a subhead. This

ad relied on the photo to make its point, forgetting that copy always should stand alone.

Figure 55 makes its point immediately. We know what is being sold and that the item is being offered at an appealing price. The headline is crystal clear and large enough to be an effective attention-getter even (or especially) reversed out. The typeface is also clear, but interesting. It has a certain warmth that is highly appropriate to the product being sold.

Figure 56 confuses the importance of the headline with the subhead. The headline should have read "Your Own Child's Drawings Reproduced on Fine Ceramic." "Today's Treasures—Tomorrow's Heirlooms" should have been the subhead. This headline forgot its main function—that of immediately identifying the item for sale. The artwork simply does not show an item common enough to be recognizable instantly as a piece of ceramic . . . let alone its main feature, that upon it is reproduced your own child's drawing.

Figure 57 features the company logo in its headline. But this particular logo implies medicine, not kitchen items with healthful overtones. Though the logo is a clever pun on the company name, puns do not necessarily clarify anything for the reader/customer, and if they do not clarify anything, they are not selling anything. More vertical space could have been available in this ad by making the name/address at the bottom two lines instead of three. The ad would have retained its visual balance, yet would have gained space for a larger head and subhead typeface.

These are interesting examples of how easily things can go awry in space advertising. Be sure you are aware of your headline's main function. Even though you do not wish a certain point to escape the customer (such as the idea previously examined, "Traditional, yet Modern"), this idea is not necessarily your headline point.

☐

85.   Are There Other Ways to Market Your Catalog?

There are many benefits to marketing your catalog through direct mail and small space ads in magazines and newspapers. But other well-known media are often overlooked for testing. The following idea-starters should give you some fresh insights and opportunities on atypical media for marketing your catalogs. Of course, just like direct mail and space, you must decide if the numbers and the audience are "right" for you before you commit to the test.

1. Community Message/Bulletin Boards. These mini "billboards" can be very cost-effective in developing a bank of prospects and customers for catalogs and name-getter products. You'll find these boards at supermarkets, chain stores and other key, high-traffic areas. Some of the more popular boards are colorful display fixtures with "take-one" holders for sales folders, booklets and flyers. Supermarket Communications Systems (Norwalk, CT) says they have over

5,500 boards in thirty-four major market areas, reaching a pass-by audience of over seventy million shoppers per week. According to SCS, catalog marketers can easily target their messages via demographic profile reports, by state, city, ZIP, neighborhood, or by individual store.

2. TV Game Shows. Several companies offer network TV game shows that are eager to give your consumer-oriented product away to contestants—along with a quick plug for your company. For catalog companies looking to supplement their marketing efforts with non-measurable advertising and promotion, this could be a low-cost mass exposure method of marketing. For example, you could give away a product with unique selling advantages, or offer a gift certificate for a "grand shopping spree" through your catalog or retail store. Game-Show Placements, Hollywood, CA, provides this service to all network shows.

3. Directories/Manuals. Catalog marketers should stroll down to their library and take a look at the many directories, manuals, guidebooks and sourcebooks that are available. Some carry advertising, even though these publications generally are *not* listed in the Standard Rate & Data books. Here is an opportunity to test several "master reference" publications used by special-interest readers. These publications usually have a long "shelf life" and a high pass-along readership. Normally you'll find either a rate card or a rate that is negotiable with the publisher.

Richard Siedlecki, Principal,
Siedlecki Direct Marketing

☐

86. More New Fields to Prospect

To keep a catalog business alive and well, new customers must constantly be developed. After pursuing routine channels for prospecting, a catalog marketer must think creatively about new methods of increasing the house list. Here are some methods that have proven effective for various companies:

1. Combine forces. When one company can't foot the bill alone, try a cooperative effort. The Sharper Image, Early Winters, Norm Thompson and Williams Sonoma combined to produce the first Discoveries catalog, now a common sight on all United Airlines flights. The goal of placing irresistible offers in front of the bored business traveler was achieved. Imagine Harry and David, Figi's and Omaha Steaks combining to produce a twelve-page mini catalog to insert in *Women's Day, Family Circle, Better Homes & Gardens,* or Brookstone, Renovators Supply and Yield House producing a joint mini catalog on the rebirth of Americana to insert in *Parade, Family Circle, Sunset, Southern Living.*

2. Cross promote. Direct response companies often lack the marketing budgets to reach wide audiences. Look for opportunities to tie your name to a "bigger hitter" in the media area. Eddie Bauer name recognition undoubtedly increased after it tied in with the Bronco II special edition by Ford Motor Company. Imagine Cabellas providing prizes for a major promotion by McDonald's, Burger King or Pizza Hut, or Gumps supplying the big reward for the winner of a bank credit card sweepstakes.

3. Use your gift certificates as incentives. Locate 10, 20 or 30 companies having major sales forces. Offer them an opportunity to use your catalog with discounted gift certificates as sales incentives. You gain volume, exposure, new customers and profits.

4. Grow your own market. Two of America's hidden markets are the college campus and the military community. Both tend to be written off because of year-to-year transiency and a perceived income shortfall. It may be time to apply a little of the British style of direct response: local reps develop their own clientele, bundle orders, receive and deliver orders for a percentage. Many of the students and soldiers will go on to be successful business people. This is a way to attract them to catalog shopping early.

5. Publicity and public relations. The direct marketing community as a whole has organized to lobby congress for postage rate fairness, fraud legislation and to improve industry wide operations. Why is there no overall program to associate the direct marketing industry with a major public program such as special olympics, minority education, cancer prevention, etc.? Who will be first to recognize the need to present direct marketing as a community-spirited business?

Because of its test/retest philosophy, the catalog business is reluctant to take big chances. To reach beyond current buyers and increase the market, more creative and daring efforts will be required.

David Rudd,
Executive Director Marketing, IFS

CHAPTER SEVEN

Telemarketing: Person-to-Person Selling

IN THE PAST FEW YEARS, TELEMARKETING HAS BECOME A key element in the catalog business.

The telemarketing professional not only takes orders and helps solve customer problems—he or she is quite literally the voice of your company.

In this chapter, you'll discover ways to get the most from your telephone staff.

☐

87. Use This Checklist to Analyze Your Telemarketing Program

To evaluate the efficiency of your telemarketing operation, ask your telemarketing supervisors these questions:

- How often are individual telemarketer reviews given regarding calls observed through the monitoring equipment? (Weekly reviews should be *minimum.*)

- How often are telephone sales training sessions conducted? Do they cover product benefits, cross-selling, up-selling, our-of-stock replacements, etc.? (Again, weekly training sessions should be *minimum.*)

- Are outbound telephone calls made to regular customers? How often?

- What outbound telephone effort is being made to follow up on initial inquiries in which no immediate sale is made?

- Are scripts being used? How often are alternate scripts tested against the control script(s)?

- What analysis has been made to review potential CRT-driven scripts, cross-selling, up-selling, out-of-stock replacements, objection handling, questions/responses, etc.?

- Has "rifle cataloging" been tested against mass catalog mailings? (Outbound phone calls to qualify; catalogs sent only to receptive prospects; outbound calls to close.)

- What back-end analysis of the telemarketing effort has been made? (Closure rates by SIC/size, size of orders by SIC/size, script comparisons, rifle vs. mass catalog marketing, part-time vs. full-time telemarketers, commissioned vs. hourly, etc.)

Unfortunately, the replies to these questions by most telemarketing supervisors/managers in business-to-business catalog telemarketing often will be "never, seldom, or haven't considered it."

Management must understand that a telemarketing operation actually can make or break their business. Professional catalog telemarketing can keep you ahead of the competition within the business-to-business market. Catalog selling must be distinctive, personalizing your corporate marketing effort.

Richard L. Bencin,
Bencin & Associates

☐

88. Making the Most of Your 800 Number

If your catalog company has a toll-free number, you have the capability to perform valuable marketing functions. But it takes personnel, training and insight into your company's marketing requirements. Four prime areas for maximizing the sales efficiency of your 800 number follow:

1. If you want people to call your 800 number only with orders, this must be prominently displayed throughout your catalog and any other advertising. State that this number is for orders only. List a separate number for customer service. Feature your 800 number on your order form, and in all your ads. Highlight the order-by-phone convenience in your copy. People respond positively to this service, especially for impulse purchases.

2. You might offer telephone customer service through a separate 800 number. Having trained individuals ready to answer questions and tackle problems can benefit you in several ways. Your public relations receives a boost. The degree of buyer confidence will increase, and with it the inclination to make repeat purchases from your company.

3. Whenever possible, close the sale on the initial incoming call, even when the respondent is only calling with an inquiry. Experience has shown that about 20 percent of incoming calls are about product information, price shopping, etc. This is where your training program really pays off. To keep costs down, you should attempt to sell on a majority of these calls. Awareness is there, interest is there—all that is required is a close.

4. A suggestion: to determine whether the 800 number truly increases sales, you should conduct A/B split testing. Run a control group (mail only) versus the group with mail plus the 800 number and measure the difference in results. Assuming a random selection of names, any difference in response would be attributed to the 800 number. You also might conduct an A/B/C test, with the A/B portion as above. The C would be a mail-plus-phone test with the consumer paying for the phone call. Over the years, L.L. Bean has conducted a variety of tests to evaluate the effectiveness of offering an 800 number. Though the company currently promotes toll-free service available seven days a week, twenty-four hours a day, other companies have found that their customers are willing to pay for the call. You should consider testing this option, especially if your product line is unique.

Ernan Roman, President,
Ernan Roman Direct Marketing

89. Effective Script Preparation for Telephone Sales

The interaction between buyer and seller on a personal, one-to-one basis is extremely fragile in telephone marketing. You'll achieve the most success when this dialogue is structured into a script to ensure consistency, quality and standardization. With this script, each prospect hears the same, carefully worded message; human error is reduced and a reliable basis for projecting results of test efforts is achieved.

Successful scriptwriting must be clear, concise, conversational and convincing. The copy must

● Avoid vague claims, half-truths and hard-sell tactics which only turn off prospects

- Anticipate questions or objections that require additional data

- Elicit and encourage response from the prospect

The following are six steps in preparing an effective script:

1. Set a limit in length. Govern this by the type of decision-maker you are contacting, and by the dollar value of the item you are selling.

2. Ask for the prospect by name. Verify that the desired person is actually on the phone.

3. Identify your communicator. Immediately upon contact with the prospect, your seller should identify himself or herself, the company and the purpose of the call.

4. Highlight the key benefits of the offer. Be sure this is done clearly and concisely.

5. Script the answers to questions the target may ask. Anticipate points that may need further explanation, as well as potential objections and problems.

6. Present the offer as an "either/or" choice. Don't make the selection too broad but present a couple of options whenever possible.

This procedure gives the communicator the necessary flexibility to establish a relaxed tone and style and determines the prospect's level of interest quickly. Test and revise each step to achieve maximum efficiency. You can test the effectiveness of your script within panels of 200 to 500 calls. Live monitoring of calls lets you control the quality of your communicators' messages and make corrections in the script. Modifications to questions and answers, style and tone can be made as the calls progress. The immediacy of the telephone allows for fast testing and retesting. Within a few hours, you can analyze and evaluate

results by keeping accurate records. You will know percentages of interest, disinterest, types of questions and objections, and the need for additional information. You will know which selling points work. And this can be further tested using split or multi-run techniques. Final scripts should be in a physical format that allows fast, easy handling by communicators. And if something is still not right, you can do a midstream test, make the necessary modifications and continue your selling effort.

Ernan Roman, President,
Ernan Roman Direct Marketing

90. The "Spike": A Quick-Hitter Promo for the Phone Room

There are times in the life of a catalog mailer when things just don't seem to go as planned. One of the most terrifying is when you are faced with catalog response rates that are just below what you'd expected. Let's say it's week number two or three after the drop, and order volume is 5 to 15 percent below what you'd planned for. You're not sure if this signals a general weakness in the catalog appeal or slow catalog distribution or some external influence like a major national election. For purity of analysis, you're tempted to "wait it out" and read the results in another week or so. But the dollar volume is just weak enough to force you to consider cutbacks in your order entry and fulfillment people. Is there anything you can do to increase dollar sales volume for a short period of time until the bigger question of catalog performance is resolved?

If you do a substantial volume by phone, the answer is yes. Use an "add-on-item/get-a-discount" promotion to spike average order size in the phone room. Here's how it works.

After the customer has completed his order, the sales representative announces that today is a very special day: if the customer adds another item, any item, to the order, there will be a 20 percent discount on the lowest-priced item in his order. The extra time to handle this explanation and promotion is generally under one minute—and the average order size can be increased by as much as 25 percent! For many companies, adding any item will cover the cost of the extra minute, as well as the discount.

This promotion can be turned on and off at will for *short* periods of time. It can recapture some of the lost dollar volume without affecting analysis of catalog response rates. Because it stimulates added item sales, this technique tends to build volume among the modestly popular items in a book. And it is broader in its appeal and easier to execute than selling specials on specific items.

Once the true nature of the sales softness is known, longer range plans can be developed. However, using the spike, you don't have to stand by and see dollar volume lag behind your plan.

David V. Rudd,
Executive Director Marketing, IFS

91. How to Rate Company Performance by Measuring Incoming Calls

One definition of a customer is "someone who buys your product/s more than once or who is willing to go through the experience again." If you find this definition acceptable, you also will find that your incoming calls will break down into two major categories, which you can track.

1. Short term revenue-related calls.
    a. Orders

    b. Sales inquiries: "how much is . . .? tell me about . . .? do you have . . .? I have this need, so can you . . .?"

Orders are immediate dollars. Sales inquiries can be converted into immediate dollars by trained representatives. Inquiries that are not able to be sold immediately but are captured as names should convert in the short term at a high rate—up to 35 percent—on subsequent mail/telephone follow-up.

2. Long term revenue-related calls.

    c. "Where's my order?"

    d. Product problems: "It doesn't work! How does it work?"

    e. Administrator problems:
        1. product not what I expected
        2. product damaged upon receipt
        3. never received
        4. bill incorrect

    f. Complaints (usually an unresolved problem)

If you don't correct these problems as they arise, you will "create" complaints and lose long-term revenue—customers! By measuring each of these categories on an ongoing basis and taking each as a percent of the total incoming customer calls (be careful not to include internal company calls in the measurements), management can get a good barometer of overall company performance. For instance, a general rule of thumb for mature companies is: if they have 50 to 60 percent short term revenue-related calls and 40 to 50 percent long term revenue-related calls, they generally are well-run organizations.

Whether or not this particular pattern is considered good or bad depends on your standards. The point is that you have specific data to interpret. A quick look at the example tells you that for every order you're getting 0.6 "where's my order?" calls. Obviously it could be one of several problems: low inventory, slow order processing, a promise of delivery time that can't be met. But the importance of categoric measurement is to furnish a control that provides a measure on which to base standards and determine the impact of short- and long-term revenue.

Example	Number	Percent
Total Calls	*1000*	*100.0*
Orders	450	45.0
Inquiries	150	15.0
		60.0% of Total
WMO (Where's my order?)	250	25.0
Product problem	60	6.0
Billing problem	88	8.8
Complaints	2	.2
		40.0% of Total

Rudolph H. Oetting, President,
R. H. Oetting & Associates, Inc.

□

92. A "Person-to-Person" Method for Reactivating Customers

There is just no substitute for the truly personal connection in any sales environment. This includes the catalog, where friendly, accommodating, knowledgeable telephone communicators and responsive, sincere, helpful customer service reps can be the lifeblood of long-term, repeat sales—the most profitable kind.

Even the most humble catalog with the simplest layout can be brought dramatically "to life" with a personalized approach to customer service. Including photos of your customer service staff in your catalog is valuable in creating the feeling that your company is warm and helpful. Adding copy (and a phone number) that suggests that these people are waiting to be of service enhances that feeling.

The importance of friendly and responsive Customer Service Reps is obvious, but they can be used in a proactive as well as a reactive way. You should have enough CSRs on staff so that each one can take about an hour a day to call inactive customers and ask how they may be of service. The CSR should have the customer's order history available when such calls are placed, and should inquire if additional merchandise of a similar or related nature is required.

If your CSRs can actually make sales, that's ideal. Even if they can't, you still can learn plenty about your customers' behavior this way. Complaints customers never bothered to lodge (but that drove them away) about delivery, merchandise, price or other problems may surface. Of course, you must have the customer's telephone number to place the call, but you should request phone numbers routinely on your order form ("in case we have to call about your order").

If a CSR makes a sale, grant a commission or bonus for reactivating the customer. In fact, give the

CSR a bonus for any sale made, whether the customer is active or inactive. Perhaps a regular customer stops placing an expected order. If an observant, conscientious CSR makes a well-timed call, this could keep a customer on the active list—a service well worth paying for.

How do you give the CSR credit for the order to distinguish it from a regular in-bound call? The simplest, most effective way is to use the honor system. Review the bonus allotments each week and keep tabs on who's getting what. You'll sniff out the rampant cheaters quickly enough, but the vast majority will be honest about it. Your willingness to trust them will be an incentive to try even harder for an "honest" sale.

Ernest H. Schell,
The Communications Center

CHAPTER EIGHT

Customer Service, Fulfillment, and the Back End

THE DIFFERENCE BETWEEN A SUCCESSFUL CATALOG business and one that fails often rests with the way it treats its customers.

Although we've touched on customer service in previous chapters, we can't stress enough that filling orders efficiently and staying in close contact with your customers creates all-important repeat business.

☐

93. Customer Satisfaction: The Bottom Line to a Repeat Mail-Order Business

Once a customer has responded to your direct mail piece, media ad or catalog, the most important factor becomes satisfaction—keeping the customer happy and buying products. How is this accomplished? There is no pat answer, but fast service, good delivery, a quality catalog and quality products are the best ingredients.

1. Fast Service. The quicker the reaction to an order, inquiry, question or complaint, the happier the customer. Consider reacting in the following ways.

a. Order. If an order can be shipped the same day it is received, it is the optimum response. Howev-

er, shipping within five days is very satisfactory to the customer.

b. Inquiries. Answer within three days, but preferably the same day. Getting a quick reply will help your customer-conversion response.

c. Questions. Answering questions about products, policy, etc., should be handled as quickly as possible. Most requests are for product information, so any delay will only delay your receipt of an order.

d. Complaints. The hardest to deal with day after day, but *so* important. Most people who bother to write a complaint are good customers. They care enough to take time to write; they generally are customers who order again and again. Answering them is top priority and a personal letter is best, but not always possible. For the quickest service, write your response on their letter and return it—they won't care. Sometimes form letters are used. No matter what response method you choose, do it fast! Same day, if possible; *never* over five days.

2. Good Delivery. Get the customer's order out the door and in the mail as fast as you can, unless otherwise requested. Choosing the shipping method is your decision. Sometimes UPS is fastest, other times, USPS. It may depend on the part of the country in which you are located. But remember—the customer will purchase more from you, if you ship quickly!

3. Quality Catalog. Basically, this means a catalog put together with your customer in mind. Make

sure product photos are clear, copy is descriptive, and that photos and copy are easily matched. Ordering information should be simple and easy to do. Options regarding printing methods, color, paper, etc., are just frosting on the cake (or budgetary considerations). Clear layout and concise information are the keys.

4. Quality Product. Be sure the quality of the product material, function, appearance and benefits correspond to what you tell the consumer to expect. Do not mislead. Photographs and illustrations must be representative, too. Then (especially if lower-priced merchandise is being sold), the customer will not be disappointed. Follow through on service, delivery and quality and you will have a whole list of satisfied customers.

□

94. How Excellent Telephone Communications Can Give You a Competitive Edge in Customer Service

Today's consumers have more—and less. They have more discretionary income, more concern for product quality and more demand for excellence in service. But they have less time than ever for shopping. This has created a golden opportunity for catalog marketers. As the industry grows, one way to gain the competitive edge is to provide excellent customer service.

How can this be achieved when the only vehicle is the telephone? The foundation of good telephone communications is knowledge of how people listen and learn. According to one study, 55 percent of what people learn is gained through body language. Forty-five percent comes from the tone of voice. Only five percent is accumulated through spoken words.

It's a shocking revelation that when a customer picks up a telephone to place an order or inquire about fulfillment, more than half of what he or she would ordinarily use to process information, draw a conclusion or develop a feeling is unavailable.

This is why it's imperative that the telephone staff identify and fully develop the tools available to them. One of the most important of those is the tone of voice. To develop an excellent telephone customer service voice, one must understand the five elements which influence tone:

- Attitude

- Smiling

- Volume

- Rate of Speech

- Inflection

Attitude, more than any other factor, influences how the telephone staff sounds. Unfortunately, when staff members consider their job, they often describe the functions they perform, and convey the mistaken attitude that "the customer is an interruption of my job." This can blemish every phone conversation. When the staff understands that the customers are the essence of the job, that will be reflected in sales conversations and generate positive customer reaction.

Smiling is the second most influential factor in the sound of the voice. When a person smiles, it raises the soft palate at the back of the mouth and creates a wider space in the front. This allows the sound waves to fluctuate more freely, making the voice more melodic. Many telemarketing firms are so convinced of the value of smiling over the phone that they have installed mirrors above sales staff desks.

Smiling sets the tone of the call from the start, making the caller feel at ease, welcomed and appreciated. Make no mistake, the customer on the other end of the line can always tell whether the salesperson is smiling.

Volume is of third importance in voice tone. Making the voice louder or softer can help control the conversation. To help calm an irrate or upset customer, the voice should be lowered. Speaking louder will help regain the attention of a customer who is confused.

Rate of speech is the fourth factor. Speaking a bit slower can help calm an angry customer or clarify a point. Telephone staff should beware of speaking too quickly, particularly when giving instructions. This can be interpreted as a lack of concern.

Inflection is the final voice factor. No customer wants to speak to an employee who talks in a machine-like monotone. Yet, when telephone staff have to give the same instructions or answers repeatedly, the chances of this happening increase. Customers hear this as a negative statement saying, "I've said this 100 times and I'm tired of repeating myself." Proper use of inflections can eliminate this problem.

When giving instructions or asking for information, the customer service person should concentrate on emphasizing key words. This generates customer interest and insures that the correct information is received.

The best technique for honing excellent telephone customer service skills is to have the staff record themselves and note the uses they're making of these factors. Repeated recording and critiques will lead to improvement. A second method is to have staff members role play telephone conversations among themselves, giving each other feedback on their effectiveness.

Excellent telephone customer service can make the critical difference between satisfied and continu-ing customers or customer dissatisfaction and lost business.

Karen Tiber,
Karen Tiber & Associates

95. Choosing Catalog Software: Inventory Control

In the same way a computer system can project sales, it can project inventory requirements based on your normal order line and early sales. Inventory projection reports show each item's quantity estimates for the length of the campaign, helping to prevent overstocking or depletions that might cause back orders.

The best computer software systems are integrated and print picking and shipping documents for available items. They automatically back order out-of-stock items for shipment when inventory is replenished. All credit card billing, invoices and credit vouchers are produced by the system.

The program should allow shipment verification either on-line or by using bar codes on package labels. If a bar code is used, the package may be scanned and weighed on a scale tied into the computer for automatic shipment verification. Either method provides positive identification of shipment for customer service and allows manifest billing for UPS.

Your computer software is the key to organizing warehouse operations for efficient order picking. During order processing, a stock picking report should be produced which totals daily requirements by item number, ensuring available quantities from bulk stock. At physical inventory time, your software should

Sample Inventory Projection Report

Item no.	Description	Cat.	Unit cost	Avg. price	To date Units	To date Sales	Projected needs Units	Projected needs Sales	On hand	On order	Required to meet projection
911	Kitchen shelving	2	6.41	18.74	1155	$21,644.70	1925	$36,074.50			
		3	6.41	18.66	65	1,212.90	108	2,015.28			
		4	6.41	18.95	1	18.95	0	00			
							2033		51	3	1979
912	Greaseless frypan	2	6.00	13.59	11	149.49	18	244.62			
		3	6.00	14.95	5	74.75	8	119.60			
							26		12	0	14

provide all the necessary documents to expedite counting.

When an item is composed of a number of components, your software should provide a connection between the components for inventory tracking. This allows one stock number to be entered when ordering a set, but checks inventory for all component items.

Software should permit multiple prices for an item in different catalogs. Prices can be charged according to the catalog from which the order was received—a real help with sales flyers.

Your software can give your customer service department an edge in handling and expediting order inquiries, providing on-line inventory verification, back order information and shipping confirmation. Inquiries should be able to be made by order number, customer name, recipient name or zip code. Inventory software can move your warehouse and shipping dock toward solid productivity gains—and solid profit gains for you.

Jim Coogan, Vice President, Woodworker's Supply
J. P. Peppler, Peppler & Associates

96. Timely Review of Inventory: The Key to Efficient Stock Control

Many years ago someone said, "Report data which is not promptly and properly reviewed is meaningless." Still a very appropriate comment. Inventory control is one area that requires rigid adherence to scheduled review of data—an area where severe cost and service problems can exist if schedules are not maintained.

When Sears, Ward and one or two other companies handled most of the mail order volume, they developed some excellent controls for their inventory activities. Though data was manually collected and tallied, their systems differed little in basic concept from what we have available today on sophisticated data processing systems.

In the old days, the merchandise manager said to the inventory controller, "Susie, every Monday morning you will get the updated stock control data covering merchandise A category. On Tuesday, category B; on Wednesday C, etc. You will review category A on

Monday and have all resultant reorders in the mail by Monday night. You will have taken reorder and follow-up actions on *all* the items in the catalog by Friday night." (Decisions were made, of course, to review certain categories on a two-week schedule, some on a three-week schedule, etc.) Records were maintained indicating that the schedules were or were not being met.

Then and now, some unbalanced stock problems result not from lack of data, but from lack of timely review. When making personal purchases by mail, we all occasionally receive the age-old message: "Sorry, we're temporarily out. Will ship soon." And serious overstock problems can and do exist in some categories of merchandise.

A subject this elementary and taken for granted can't be a problem, can it? Attention catalogers: money can be saved and better service achieved if schedules for reviewing inventory control activity are developed and maintained on a timely basis.

R. Roy Hedberg, President,
Hedberg & Associates, Inc.

97. Out of Stock, Out of Mind? The Long-Term Impact of Canceling a Customer Order

Canceling a customer order has a concrete effect on future order response. The following models dramatically illustrate just how much revenue is lost when orders are canceled.

In this model, we have established certain assumptions regarding our hypothetical catalog mailing.

1. Response rates are valid and representative over time (i.e., there is not seasonality).

2. We'll analyze a three-year period and won't include markdowns or returns.

3. For simplicity, mailings will be said to occur at even, regular intervals (the beginning of every three-month period, with income received at the end of the three-month period).

4. Cancellation occurs one time only, in order to let us monitor the effect of cancellation has on a first and only purchase, not multiple cancellations on the same customer.

For variable assumptions, we'll use: (a) a constant average order of $100, (b) a constant cost of capital at 4 percent per year, and (c) a constant gross margin of 20 percent.

Using these assumptions, let's create the response path using 5,000 most recent customers and examine the results. First, we'll see what happens if we *do* fill the orders and *always* fill the orders. Then we'll cancel those orders, but fill any future response orders. Let's examine our findings and see how the first few mailing results are derived.

In the no-cancel model (Table 1), we start at time $t+0$ with 5,000 customers who all received their orders and subsequently respond in mailing $t+1$ at a rate of 10 percent. So in mailing $t+1$ we have 500 orders at $100 each, netting $10,000 gross margin dollars, using 20 percent as our gross margin rate.

Table 1. No-Cancel Model of Mailings and Response

Time	Rate	$t+0$	$t+1$	$t+2$	$t+3$
$t-1$	10.0%	5,000	500	50 + 437	49 + 44 + 325
$t-2$	9.7%		4,500	450	438
$t-3$	8.0%			4,064	406
$t-4$	7.0%				3,738

	$t+0$	$t+1$	$t+2$	$t+3$
Orders	5,000	500	487	417
Resp $	$500,000	$50,000	$48,650	$41,738
*FV net profit	$100,000	$10,000	$9,730	$8,348
*PV net profit	$100,000	$9,901	$9,538	$8,101

Table 2. One-Cancel Model of Mailings and Response

Cancel rate	$t+0$	$t+1$	$t+2$	$t+3$
$t-1$ 4.5%	5,000			
$t-2$ 3.9%		4,775		
$t-3$ 3.6%			4,589	
$t-4$ 3.5%				4,424
No-cancel rate				
$t-1$ 10.0%		225	23 + 186	21 + 20 + 165
$t-2$ 9.7%			203	188
$t-3$ 8.0%				184

Table 3. Results from First Three Mailings

	$t+0$	$t+1$	$t+2$	$t+3$
Orders filled	0	225	209	206
Resp $	$0	$22,500	$20,873	$20,571
FV profit	$0	$4,500	$4,175	$4,114
PV profit	$0	$4,455	$4,092	$3,993

*FV = Future Value
*PV = Present Value

Table 4. Comparative Results

	no-cancel	one-cancel
Orders filled $t+0$	5,000	0
Orders filled $t+1$		
through $t+12$	3,660	2,050
Total orders filled	8,660	2,050
PV net profit $t+0$	$100,000	$0
PV net profit $t+0$		
through $t+12$	$69,524	$38,730
Total PV net profit	$169,524	$38,730

Now, in mailing $t+2$ we have 500 most recent purchasers who, at a rate of 10 percent, contribute fifty orders. We also have 4,500 customers who last bought $t-2$ quarters ago and respond at a rate of 9.7 percent, which gives us an additional 437 orders. Total orders for this mailing are 487.

In mailing $t+3$ we have these 487 most recent buyers who respond at the best rate of 10 percent. We have 450 who respond at 9.7 percent. We have 4,064 who respond at 8 percent. And so on.

The one-cancel model (Table 2) is a little more complex due to the use of two response curves. The 5,000 customers whose orders we canceled respond only at a 4.5 percent rate of 225 orders. But in the $t+1$ mailing during the next quarter, these 225 customers respond at the best no-cancel rate of 10 percent.

Results from the first three mailings are in Table 3; the bottom line after three years' mailings is in Table 4.

If we never cancel on these 5,000 orders, we can expect an additional 3,660 orders over the three-year period. If we cancel those 5,000 (even if we never cancel again), we can expect 2,050 orders. Given the stipulated variable assumptions, this translates to a loss of $30,794 over and above the $100,000 which is obvious.

Basically what you can calculate is how much you're going to lose in future orders if you must cancel orders now. All you need are

- estimated response curves

- timing of mailings

- average dollar of orders (not necessarily constant)

- profit margin

- discount rates (constant or otherwise)

You can use this information as motivation to do everything you can in your own operation to avoid order cancellations. And you can educate suppliers as to the real cost of canceling customer orders, encouraging these sources to work carefully and rapidly in reordering merchandise. What you lose, they lose too!

Judy Staschover,
I. Magnin

□

98. How to Write Collection Letters That Work

If a sale isn't a sale until it's a paid-in-full, then why is it that catalog marketers put all of their creative talent and emphasis on the front end of their direct marketing programs? Isn't it just possible that if a little more creative time was spent on the back end, a more profitable program would exist?

There are at the very least 200 creative ways to ask for payment in full. And direct marketers can probably find another 200 ways to say "pay what you owe—now!" You've worked hard to persuade that customer to buy; how hard have you worked to persuade him to pay?

Okay—so the back end of your catalog marketing program doesn't get your creative expertise or attention. You don't have time; you're not interested; you have an accountant; you have a lawyer; you have an accounts receivable department; you have a collection department. But, truthfully, have you ever read a creative dunning letter from a lawyer or an accountant? And if your accounts receivable and collection areas were truly creative, then you wouldn't have any bad debt factor. Creativity in collection sells the benefit of getting paid, but you've got to do it with sizzle and timing.

Most collection letters still use the language and graphics of the 50s and 60s. How many times in dunning correspondence can you use the words: obligation, trust, honor, fulfill, credit, payment, settlement, prompt and immediate? And even some of those words are frowned upon by the FTC. I like words like: tight, hard times, asset, action, future deal, offer, tough, fast and impact.

Most collection letters are boring and the more letters you send, the more boring they become. Some collection letters are never opened because the envelopes are recognizable, look alike, and are equally boring. But if you used some of the creative concepts you developed for selling your products on the back end of your system, you would see marked improvement. Use graphics, use colored envelopes, change your collection approach often. If you don't have the time or in-house talent to develop a back-end creative collection program, contact a collection pro who can give you time and talent.

It's a new year in which to get paid for the products you sell. The economy may give catalog marketers a difficult time generating payments. So think about new collection tactics, do a better job on your up-front credit screening (zip clusters) and take time to look at the back end of your system. Without a strong back end, the front end doesn't work.

David Klein, North Shore Agency

☐

CHAPTER NINE

Measuring Your Success

It all ends up on the bottom line. In this final chapter we've included some thoughts on what makes a success in the catalog business, and how to be sure you're staying on the right track.

☐

Figure 58

99. You Can Turn Catalog Problems into Profit-makers

There's nothing like a crisis or unsurmountable problem to bring out the best in a truly creative catalog marketer. What follows are some tips on how consumer and business-to-business catalogs solve those big problems with simple and profitable solutions.

Several years ago Halls, an upscale fashion and gift catalog then owned by Hallmark, printed the wrong 800 number in its catalog. Nope, it wasn't just a one-time, one-page typo—it was wrong throughout forty-eight pages. And the error wasn't found until *after* the books were printed and bound. All 500,000 of them. What would you do if you were faced with the same dilemma?

For starters, the general manager of the Halls catalog did the obvious and tried to get AT&T to assign them the 800 number they'd published. No luck; it was already in use. Then he had another idea that ended up *increasing* phone orders to the correct 800 number.

Halls cheshired an "OOOPS . . . WE GOOFED!" label with the correct 800 number right across the front of their beautiful four-color cover (see Figure 58). While the art director may not have been happy, the label caught customers' eyes and generated a record number of phone orders. Problem solved; Halls' sales soared.

Not long ago, Haver Veterinary Supplies was putting together its big annual 72-page catalog. The book was at the printer and headed for the bindery when, at the last minute, Haver decided to offer a special Early Bird discount. What would you do?

This time the solution was a simple brown kraft catalog wrap (see Figure 59) that was written, typeset, printed and delivered literally overnight. It featured a strong promotional headline, "NEW CATALOG—SPECIAL SAVINGS OFFER," and followed up with details about discounts and deadlines. This wrap may not have been as attractive as the catalog cover beneath it, but it significantly increased sales. Plus, it generated much earlier orders to even out the peaks and valleys in Haver's annual catalog sales.

Figure 59

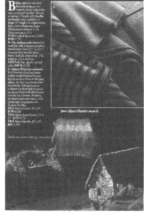

Figure 60

Figure 61

Another problem many catalog marketers face is how to substantiate a key product benefit that needs to be experienced firsthand by the customer. In other words, how can a catalog duplicate the experience of touching and feeling?

The Peruvian Connection, purveyors of imported handmade alpaca fashions and goods, found an effective solution to this problem. From the very start, owners Annie and Biddy Hurlbut knew they had to find a way to give credibility to the claim that their alpaca really was cashmere-soft without the cashmere price. They could say it a dozen different ways, but the customer really had to touch an alpaca sweater to believe it. The solution? They included an alpaca swatch (see Figure 60) on page 3 of the catalog.

The next problem was how to glue in the swatch, since it couldn't be machine-affixed. Annie and Biddy recruited the local high school football team to do the gluing and sticking as a team fundraiser. The swatch must be working because they continue to include it in all their catalogs. Whether or not the football team is still doing the job isn't clear!

Now there's another catalog, Landau—The World's Most Beautiful Woolens—using the same technique to introduce its machine-washable-and-dryable Superwash wool shirts. Just in case you don't believe what you read about these shirts, you can test the claims for yourself by washing and drying the 2″ square swatch included on a half-page insert inside the back cover (see Figure 61).

Next time you're faced with a catalog problem, a crisis, or an unexpected shift in plans, take a tip from these folks and look at your situation as an opportunity to be creative and increase sales.

Pat Friesen, Executive Vice President,
Schmid & Associates

100. Determine and Control Costs: It's the Only Way You'll Target Profits

What portion of each dollar of sales received "in the door" should be spent for advertising, merchandise, operations and accounting? The answer can be simply stated, but is not meaningful until there is complete understanding of how actual costs are being allocated to the areas involved. There are major variations, company to compay, on allocation decisions.

Advertising costs should truly represent *all* costs of getting one dollar of business "in the door." This includes all catalog preparation costs (in-house and out-of-house, layout, photography, copy, etc.), all costs of printing (including paper, all mailing costs and postage), and all costs in-house and out-of-house for media advertising, package inserts, and so forth.

Proper cost allocations must consider how much of the Chairman's, President's, and Officers' payroll costs should be charged to advertising. What portions of computer department costs should be charged? What specific costs are involved with maintaining the customer name file?

Merchandise costs are easier to identify. These include delivered costs of merchandise received, payroll costs for inventory control, merchandise report analysis, reordering and a portion of computer costs charged to the merchandise control segment.

Accounting department costs are normally easily identified—but they also must receive their proper allocations of computer, other equipment and space costs.

The fulfillment section of operations should include all payroll costs applicable to receiving, processing and shipping customer orders, and to receiving and warehousing inventory. Again, allocate for computer and other equipment costs, including space costs. And, as for all accounts, allocate for taxes other than taxes on profits. Costs of money must also be allocated to all accounts, as appropriate.

Generally speaking, a catalog mail-order operation should operate with advertising costs of 38%, merchandise 40%, operations 10%, accounting 2%. This provides a 10% profit before taxes.

Advertising vs. merchandising vs. operational costs will vary considerably depending on Average Order Value. As many companies have discovered, particularly in the past few years, it is difficult to gain a profit if the overall Average Order Value is not constantly increasing, at least staying abreast of inflation. An Average Order Value of $60 vs. $25 will have a major effect on costs in all areas.

Another variable is how much you must spend annually for replacements and additions to your Customer Name File. The annual loss of an active file involving 400,000 names is about 20 percent, or 80,000 names. Replacement costs for 80,000 names are usually much less per name than replacement costs for 8,000 names.

A major cost factor played with month-to-month is commonly called Prepaid Advertising Costs. Example: a January 31st P/L statement is being prepared. A catalog mailing of perhaps 50,000 books occurred the first week in January. A certain dollar sales response has been received. How does this early response relate to the total response anticipated during January, February, March, April? What portion of the perhaps $15,000 catalog cost should be charged to the January P/L? Unfortunately, the answer is sometimes "How good do I want January to look?" If underallocation is made to January, the piper still has to be paid. An important question: who makes that decision?

True assessments of costs cannot be made and properly directed corrective actions cannot be taken without proper allocation of costs. If total costs are too high, is it truly because it costs too much to get business "in the door"? Or does it properly lie in the many areas of getting business "out the door" including, incidentally, the Customer Service Department? Most failures involve spending too much getting business "in the door." But there are many instances of improper expenditures of payroll, equipment and supply costs in all areas other than advertising.

R. Roy Hedberg, President,
Hedberg & Associates, Inc.

101. How to Analyze a Catalog's Profitability

Successful catalog marketing is not easy; mail order merchandising is a complicated business. Understanding each facet of the business is a key to control, and the catalog manager must be able to see these facets "at a glance." It is critical to keep the three key variables in establishing and maintaining a successful catalog marketing program at or near the minimum required level. All other variables can be controlled and managed if these three are strong

1. Response rate

2. Average order size

3. Gross margin

Let's suppose that your catalog has a healthy response rate, average order size and gross margin. How should you be analyzing your book to fine-tune it and improve each effort? Your first step in analyzation is to look at the following factors and use the information to make the next book more responsive and profitable.

When a catalog life is over or when results in hand allow you to project sufficiently, take a copy of the catalog and list beside each photograph the units sold and dollars of revenue for each item. Then, at the top of the page put the *total dollars for that page*. This simple exercise shows which products work and which do not and shows everyone connected with the catalog how each product and each square inch of space has performed.

Upon completion of the page-by-page markup, a sales contributoin by page can be prepared. This analysis tells which pages are pulling in sales and which are not. Since pages usually contain a single category of products, the sales by page can also show which product categories are selling. Example:

Sales Contribution by Page

Page	General description	Sales	% Total	Rank
2	Luggage	$14,608	1.3%	30
3	Luggage	$105,920	9.6%	1
4	Exercise & fitness	$44,628	4.0%	8
5	Exercise & fitness	$47,407	4.3%	6

The sales of some pages are affected by the placement of that page. Consequently, the items you place on key pages must be carefully chosen. Best pages in a catalog are, in order, the back cover, the inside front spread, the inside back spread, and the middle spread that's split by the staples and the order form. (Some catalogers experience more strength from the middle spread than the inside back spread.) Most catalogers find that the other spreads perform about the same.

The next key information for analysis is the ranking of merchandise in the catalog by best-selling dollars, best-selling units, and gross profit. These rankings drive the merchandising decisions for the next book. All three rankings are necessary. In the typical catalog you have some items that are stars in terms of revenue generated; some items with lower price points that deliver less revenue but a large volume of unit sales. There are also products that deliver only fair amounts of dollars or units but have margins so good that the items bear repeating. Example:

Best Selling Dollars

Item	Revenue	Units sold	Gross profit
1. Exercycle	$22,167	61	$11,250
2. Book light	$20,806	221	$9,861
3. Carry-on bag	$18,272	81	$8,889
4. Emergency flasher	$14,070	99	$7,012
5. Manicure set	$12,995	116	$6,091
6. Travel alarm clock	$10,442	39	$5,888

Use these techniques for data collection and analysis to clarify and simlify the operation and planning of your catalog.

Jim Coogan, Vice President, Woodworker's Supply